KEEP GOING

NAVIGATING THE *NEXT BIG* STEPS IN YOUR LIFE

BILL ISAACS

Unless otherwise indicated, Bible quotations are from the NEW LIVING TRANSLATION.

For information, contact the author by email:
bill@forwardleadership.org

ISBN: 978-1-59684-751-4

Keep Going

By: Bill Isaacs

Printed in the United States of America

BOOKS BY BILL ISAACS

Life is Harder Than We Thought (Derek Press 2011)
When Leaves Turn Under (Derek Press 2010)
A Life Worth Living (Derek Press 2009)
What Our Storms Teach Us (Derek Press 2006)
Invited To the Deep End (Pathway Press 2004)
Intersections (Xulon Press 2003)
Embracing Destiny (Pathway Press 2002)
For other books and resources available from this author
visit: *www.forwardleadership.org*

FOREWORD

Bill Isaacs brings an unusual perspective to his life as a Christ-follower—and to his work as a minister—and so to this book. It is a book, essentially, about pushing forward into the future. Everyone of us does that every day. Every new morning is a kind of unknown, bringing with it both the promise of a new beginning and the hazards of unmarked territory. What will the day bring forth?

It is said that Yogi Berra, that oft-quoted baseball coach of an earlier period, once said: "It's hard to make predictions, especially about the future." Indeed it is. Even for Christian believers, who trust that the future is in God's hands, moving into tomorrow's unknown terrain with confidence and energy can be hard. We like to know what lies ahead. We trust the familiar. We want to do what we have done before. To paraphrase Berra: "It's hard to move forward, especially into the future. . . ."

And sometimes, it's harder than others. Bill Isaacs knows about those times. He was the administrative bishop of the Churches of God in Louisiana when the hurricane Katrina swept through the lower half of that state in 2005, leaving devastation and chaos in its path. As I watched, from the safe vantage point of unscathed East Tennessee, Bill began reaching out to his churches, his pastors, his hurting congregations, comforting, encouraging, coordinating support efforts at a practical level.

This, I thought, is church leadership. Not just drafting ecclesiastical resolutions or managing small bureaucracies, but being a pastor to pastors, a clear voice of optimism and hope when things have gone badly wrong. Solving problems. Moving forward.

That was an important part of Bill's life experience. Not only was I watching, but many others throughout the Church of God were also. I think that was the time when a broader public began to see Bill Isaacs as an exceptional leader.

By his side during those six years in Louisiana was Kathy, his effervescent and vibrant wife. She was "all in" for the many years she and Bill worked together in ministry. They weren't just married, they were joined at the hip. But in that perverse way life has of taking away what it gives, Bill had to learn to live—and to lead—without her. She was diagnosed with cancer, and in March 2011, Bill and his sons released her into the eternal care of the Lord.

Kathy's battle with illness captured the imagination of people all across the nation. Bill and the family made a decision to be as transparent as possible about the whole journey, and as a result, multiplied thousands of people followed the story of her courageous battle and the path her family travelled, before and beyond that terrible loss.

Bill has written about that entire experience, and this new book is not about Kathy. To some degree, however, it is inseparable from Kathy, just as it is inseparable from Katrina and all the other parts of Bill's life which have required "moving forward" into an unknowable future. Part of his communicative gift is his willingness to be autobiographical without being self-absorbed, and that gift infuses and animates this book.

Bill is a graduate of Lee University, but not a typical one. He began as a young minister, the son of a minister, who came to Lee torn between the "call to preach" and the "call to prepare." In his case, as with many passionate young people, the urgency to enter ministry won out, and he left college to become a full-time evangelistic, but not without making a promise to his mother that he would someday finish his degree.

That story is common enough, but rarely is the promise fulfilled, certainly not when a young man's ministry is as productive and highly regarded as Bill's became. But he never forgot the promise to his mother, and eventually, as a respected church leader, he resumed his studies in Lee's distance-learning program and completed a BA degree in Pastoral Studies in 2007. What most impressed me about all that is that Bill, when his degree was finished, decided to come to campus, put on a cap-and-gown, get in the graduation line with all those young twenty-somethings, and walk across the stage to shake my hand and receive his diploma. He didn't want to just quietly sneak over the finish line. He wasn't embarrassed that his journey to graduation took 32 years. He wanted the whole trip. That was classic Bill Isaacs

Bill Isaacs is a bridge-builder. He is widely regarded as being one of the key players in bridging the generational divide in his denomination. He is old enough at 55 to be a veteran leader, but young enough to be part of the new wave of innovation and creative ideas in the church. His close relationship with two sons, Jason and Jeremy, both of whom are bright and effective ministers themselves, no doubt provides a big part of that equation. I have rarely known a leader who is more trusted by men and women on all sides of the various generational issues.

I believe you will enjoy this book, not because it is about Bill Isaacs—it isn't about him, really—but because it is about you and me. He is an insightful and interesting commentator on his own experiences and on the message of scripture. But the book is not about him; it's about all those times when each of us must choose whether to hunker down in some kind of static state, or to move forward into the brilliant and unforeseen future God has prepared for us.

I have found this book insightful and inspiring, and I'm confident you will too!

Paul Conn
President, Lee University
Cleveland, TN

After the death of Moses the Lord's servant, the Lord spoke to Joshua son of Nun, Moses' assistant. He said, "Moses my servant is dead. Therefore, the time has come for you to lead these people, the Israelites, across the Jordan River into the land I am giving them. I promise you what I promised Moses: 'Wherever you set foot, you will be on land I have given you—from the Negev wilderness in the south to the Lebanon mountains in the north, from the Euphrates River in the east to the Mediterranean Sea in the west, including all the land of the Hittites.' No one will be able to stand against you as long as you live. For I will be with you as I was with Moses. I will not fail you or abandon you. "Be strong and courageous, for you are the one who will lead these people to possess all the land I swore to their ancestors I would give them. Be strong and very courageous. Be careful to obey all the instructions Moses gave you. Do not deviate from them, turning either to the right or to the left. Then you will be successful in everything you do. Study this Book of Instruction continually. Meditate on it day and night so you will be sure to obey everything written in it. Only then will you prosper and succeed in all you do. This is my command—be strong and courageous! Do not be afraid or discouraged. For the Lord your God is with you wherever you go." Joshua then commanded the officers of Israel, "Go through the camp and tell the people to get their provisions ready. In three days you will cross the Jordan River and take possession of the land the Lord your God is giving you." (*Joshua 1:1-11 NLT*)

DEDICATION

The moments that mark my life with greatest joy are those with my sons, their wives and the amazing grandchildren who are God's gifts to me. In some ways, the motivation of my life to keep going beyond everything has come from the realization that I'm accountable and connected to an amazing family and my heart's desire is to walk honorably before them and inspire them to follow Christ.
I humbly dedicate this book to:

Jeremy
Jason
Corrie
Andrea
Cooper
Branson
Sadie Hope
Tucker
Kinley Grace
Norah Faith

CONTENTS

SPECIAL THANKS . . .

I'm humbled to have people in my life who daily contribute to my well being and help me advance the projects and efforts that my heart is connected to. This project, as much as any other is the collection of so many who deserve at least the simple mention of thanks for the record.

Pat and Jan Wright have been as much family to me in the past three years as one could possibly know. Our journey has been filled with deep emotional moments, incredible laughter and joy. We have prayed and planned together much of what is now OneOhio and the amazing thing is we did not know we would be here. Destiny marked us for the path we now walk. I trust you and your covering over my life is never taken for granted.

Doris Fuson has been my personal assistant now for five years and each year she gets better and better at what she does. The load she carries is enormous and I marvel at her gift for grace under pressure and for the skill to keep all the details organized in a way that allows our mission in OneOhio to be accomplished. I'm so very thankful for the position you hold in my life.

My staff and leadership teams in OneOhio have been so giving, sacrificing much for the dreams we hold together. To be surrounded by the visionary and courageous people who lead OneOhio is a daily blessing. We have simply chosen not to be afraid to experiment. Time will tell the tale but for these past three years, it has been exhilarating.

My friends at Derek Press are always to be valued for the way they allow me to work alongside them to get the finished product we desire. Thanks Jerry Puckett and your team for another wonderful partnership.

During the writing of this project, I picked up a copy of John Eldredge's book, *Desire* and through the months afterward, I read, read and reread the book, marking it thoroughly and from the pages came life-changing truth. I've never met John but I want the record to reflect how much his book changed my view of life with Christ and how much God used it to help me see inside of me.

FROM ME . . .

"Moses my servant is dead. Therefore, the time has come for you to lead these people, the Israelites, across the Jordan River into the land I am giving them." [1]

The announcement startled me when I read it. It is direct and weighted. It must have felt that way to Joshua as well. Moses was his teacher, mentor and spiritual father. In truth, Joshua's identity and leadership is rooted in the man whom God has just announced was dead. For decades, Joshua has been a faithful assistant to Moses and you cannot walk in the company of great people and not be deeply impacted by their loss and absence. While he has been witness to some amazing miracles but has never been the leader . . . until now.

Is he ready? Can he do it without Moses? Questions of confidence and competency are obvious for him and the people. Moses has been the leader of these people from the beginning and now the new leader is about to embark.

What will change?

How will the people relate to him?

These are the same questions that Joshua is asking himself. They are natural responses to the human dilemma of

---

1 Joshua 1:2 (NLT)

accepting the assignments God has chosen to give us in view of life's unexpected and devastating moments. The death of my wife a few years ago, forced me to see life differently and to embrace a future I had seldom considered possible. In the days that followed, it would be God's call that I should *keep going* with my own life, even though it would mean my life would continue without the one who had walked the path of life with me for more than three decades.

Joshua knows that feeling. Life without Moses is not only unimaginable but the call to go forward without those who have shared our path and made such life investments in us requires a courage that we may feel we don't possess. Just a few months later, I remember wondering about my own life assignment again, in light of the death of a great man, Walter Atkinson, who had taught me so much. *Who would I go to for the coaching and advice he had so patiently given down through the years?* We served and did life together over several decades and his trust and confidence allowed me to soar but there was always an emotional safety net and now his death hit me squarely in the pit of my stomach . . . I was going to go on without him. *Could I do that? Can you?*

However, there is no way to know, unless you keep going.

Movement.

I'm convinced the confidence Joshua needs and the people require is found in the obedience of movement. Without movement, there is no way to predict if anything will work or if anyone is capable to keep going. Generally we like secure things and so we need reassurance that often will not come until we move.

- Peter never walks on the water until he steps out from the boat.

- The lame man is not healed until he picks up his bed and walks as Jesus commanded.
- The water is not changed to wine unless the disciples do as the Lord instructed.

Joshua does have some things going for him according to Numbers 27:12-22:

- The Spirit of God rests upon him. . . .
- He was publicly commissioned by Moses to succeed him. . . .
- The authority of Moses has been transferred to him in the presence of the people so they know. . . .
- Most of all, God has **chosen** him.

That would seem to be the concluding point—the absolute confidence of God in us and selection of us despite our moments and journey. His call is for us to keep going toward the future He has planned. Yet, the task is daunting and one cannot help but imagine the emotions at work in Joshua's heart to hear God say . . . *"The time has come for you to lead these people . . ."* The trigger is the startling announcement of God—*"Moses is dead."* Moses' death is a signal that things that once were are no more and that it is time to move. I have been hearing that same call. It came this morning in a hotel room more than 4,000 miles from my home. From my sleep, I awoke to the whisper in my spirit . . . it's time—get moving! The only other choice is to remain stuck in the quagmire of what once was and forfeit the chance to experience what He has chosen.

The people who came out of Egypt were a moving people. It was a daily ritual to watch for the cloud of God's Presence move and when it started moving—the people packed up and started. Sometimes I've wondered if that were not an easier way than today. We just allow some physical sign to hover near our lives and as it moves, we move. Today, we are guided and directed by the Holy Spirit and the tendency we have is to remain in our same places, despite the Spirit's prompting.

Joshua and the people now have the mandate, and it's time to move into the land that God had promised to Abraham, to Isaac and to Jacob hundreds of years before. The Promised Land was theirs but they would have to move to obtain it.

Therein lies our problem.

The movement of God is always forward. He is always working in us with emphasis on where we are and where we are going. Unless there is an issue of sinfulness or correction, God seldom seems to deal with the issues or events of the past. He gently pushes us to look forward and to move ahead. It is our tendency, on the other hand, to focus too much attention on the things behind us, what we left behind or to misrepresent how much we valued the former things.

- Lot's wife was destroyed because she disobeyed the command "Don't look back!"
- The Children of Israel often would complain about wanting to go back to Egypt.
- As change comes to our own world, we relish the memories of our past so much we long to return to what was.

There's no going back. God will not allow it. We are destined to go forward.

This is a book about movement toward the things God has chosen for our future and not our past. It is a call that this is not the time to reminisce about what once was but to dream about what can be and to listen for the call of God's spirit to advance.

In the Spring of 1999, I sat in a church and heard God's call to dream bigger dreams and begin to think larger thoughts for my own life. One of the results of my commitment to that call was my public writing career and what you hold in your hand is my obedience to the call of God to move from where I was to where He is taking me. While driving Ohio state route 30 in the early winter of 2011, I felt the nudge of God's spirit to "keep going!" It was a significant moment for me given where I had just come from and the trap of fear and intimidation about the future. However, there was no doubt in my heart that this project would come and it would come from the ashes of what felt like life's most crushing blow. Yet, life continues and I'm alive and in that reality is God's call—keep going!

This past Sunday morning, I spoke to 150 pastors and church planters in Brasilia, Brazil about God's call to lead others to faith and the entrusting of such an important assignment to men and women who are weak and fragile in so many ways. It is that trust God has in us that is so weighty. We fear because we know how incapable we are. He persists because He knows how accomplished we can be when we trust and believe in Him and by doing so, in our own futures! One of the reasons He insists we keep going beyond our former moments is that He knows what lies ahead and like a parent who cannot wait for the child to open the gift, God is excited for you and I to embrace the future and experience the things only He could have arranged for our lives.

I don't pretend to understand much about God these days; in fact, I'm convinced that some of what I formerly was sure about is now a new mystery to me. The moments when I think I have figured out how God works and how He moves within my existence, I come to new places and experiences which tell me I don't have a clue! Life has been cruel to us at times and the surprises have taken our collective breath away and we want to hide away and spend our remaining days in safe and predictable places. Yet, we were not called or redeemed to be predictable! Nor was God's design that we hide until our lives are ended. Rather, His call is to great risk and opportunity and while we don't yet realize the depth of it all, the moments and experiences of our past have only positioned us for what is to come!

So how do we navigate our new normal and how do we embrace the grace to start over and keep going?

One step
One day
One faithful obedience at a time!

We cannot linger in the graveyards of our painful past, nor languish in the memories of greater glories. Tomorrow summons us and we must respond.

Keep Going!
Bill Isaacs
2012

MOVEMENT

The time has come for you to lead these people, the Israelites, across the Jordan River into the land I am giving them.[2]

2   Joshua 1:1 NLT

The movement of water fascinates me. In part, I think it is so because water moves at a pace all its own and even when we try to control its flow, we are not always successful. Take the movement of water under my driveway as an example. Trying to stay ahead of the moisture and water is frustrating me because it freezes in winter, breaking up the concrete in my drive and requiring the expenditure of funds to fix and repair. So, my friend, Tom works to clear out the broken concrete, fill in the cracks and seal the surface against further water damage only to find that in short order, the water has resurfaced in another place and more damage is incurred. We have sought to force the water away from the drive and into a nearby ditch but then the water moved to other areas and more cracks appeared. The water seems to have a mind of its own.

The Colorado River is a cherished place for the rafters in the West, who seek to tame the rapids and energy of the water racing through the canyons. It is no small task to navigate the raging rushing waters and there is danger in each of the dips, turns or cascades the river offers. I've never had the privilege to ride the rapids there but I've watched the action and it is both thrilling and awe inspiring. While it is recreation and enjoyment, there is an ominous warning of caution to those who would seek to tame the rapids and the violent potential of swiftly moving water.

However, engineers have learned how to marshal the movement of water and to harness it for public good. Dams and power plants dot the landscape for the purpose of using the movement of water for things like the energy needed to make this laptop computer fire up and work for typing this manuscript! Hydro-electric power formed from the movement of water has been a vital link to the establishment of communities, homes and local businesses. When controlled, it is clear the movement of water can be useful to better our lives and creating scenic lakes and recreational resorts.

When the movement of water is not so controlled, the devastation can be deadly. I remember in 1976 when I was living in Colorado, the Big Thompson Canyon flood near Greeley, Colorado killed many people in that resort camping area from flash flood waters rising more than 10-15 feet high that crashed upon unsuspecting campers. I lived in Louisiana during the devastating events of Hurricane Katrina and talked with eyewitnesses to the storm surge of more than twenty feet that came into St. Bernard Parish from the Gulf of Mexico when the storm made landfall. During the height of that storm, I also recall how the winds drove the waters of Lake Ponchatrain into the city of New Orleans and flooded the Ninth Ward neighborhoods with waters as deep as seventeen feet. The uncontrolled movement of water can be deadly.

There is power in movement!

After announcing that the legendary Moses was dead, God's command to Joshua was to start moving the people toward their intended destination. In fact, the actual command was that it was time to begin the process—to get moving beyond their present place. Though they were coming out of a traumatic season, they were not to linger in the drama of Moses' passing or remain fixated on their present location. Their orders were to move ahead and embrace the future. The choice was clear. Remain and die or move and live—as God intended.

Not much has changed in the years since that command came to Joshua. God continues to call each of us to keep moving beyond our present moments, toward our future. If we remain too long here, in this place, in this moment, we may eventually die. We are on a journey to our destiny. We were created for the movement of our lives in harmony with God's purposes. These present environments and experiences are not the final chapters of who we are called to be but we must keep going in order to get there.

Remember this, the movement of God is always forward . . . never backward or for that matter, standing still. Even though there will be times that we should stand still and wait, the call of God ultimately to us is to stay in movement with His plans, calls and purposes. That is not always easy. These present places can be tempting to us. Sometimes even our weariness with life seems to beckon us to remain and stay in this place rather than put forth the effort to advance. Be careful that you are not held captive to the siren call of this place where you find yourself now or the former places you have been, to the point that you forfeit the plans God has arranged for your life.

Just today I was thinking about the Children of Israel and how often and quickly they reverted to wanting to return to Egypt. Anytime they met opposition, faced a challenging moment, feared that they might suffer, they would cry out that they wished they had remained in Egypt. Is that not amazing? Remember how Moses came to be called at the burning bush? God said,

> "I have certainly seen the oppression of my people in Egypt. I have heard their cries of distress because of their harsh slave drivers. Yes, I am aware of their suffering. So I have come down to rescue them from the power of the Egyptians and lead them out of Egypt into their own fertile and spacious land. It is a land flowing with milk and honey . . . Look! The cry of the people of Israel has reached me, and I have seen how harshly the Egyptians

abuse them. Now go, for I am sending you to Pharaoh. You must
lead my people Israel out of Egypt."[3]

It was because of their cries and anguish that God responded in the first place; yet they consistently felt they were better off in Egypt than they were in the movement of God's plan to bring them to the land of Promise!

If that sounds familiar, it should because we are often the same way. We say we want God to do amazing things in us, to use our lives for greatness but when the pressure is on, we often crave the comfortable surroundings of our former places. We forget that those places were not comfortable either, that in our hearts we crave the movement of God, we want the progress of our lives to be transformed by God's power and grace. Yet to get there, we have to move from where we are to the new places.

My father was a pastor and I moved a lot. We spent about 1-2 years in most of those early smaller churches where my father was appointed. It became second nature to be in a new school every few years, to have new friends and be adjusting to new environments often. Looking back, I know that those experiences shaped me because they forced me to adjust. Others of you have lived in the same house and attended the same church your whole life and to think of moving away and starting over has high levels of anxiety written all over it. Now, I'm not advocating moving for moving sake and for the record, I hate moving. The larger point is our willingness to go, to move when God calls and when it serves the purpose of God.

Abraham was called by God to leave his comfortable surroundings and move to the place where God would show

3 Exodus 4:7-10 NLT

him. Talk about a life of uncertainty, Abraham left home
and had no forwarding address! It is amazing to me that
Sarah his wife went with him. I don't know many women
like that who would pick up stakes and move without a plan,
but she did. They both did and God used their obedience to
birth a new nation from which God would send His Son for
the redemption of the whole world.

I'm struck by the instruction Joshua gave to the people as
they prepare to move across the Jordan River and on to the
conquest of Jericho. The people have spent the larger part of
their lives in the mode of the journey through the wilderness
and desert. It's all they have ever known. This new call and
journey will be different. Yet that is not bad—it is in fact,
very good. Joshua reminds them. . . .

Early the next morning Joshua and all the Israelites left
Acacia Grove and arrived at the banks of the Jordan River,
where they camped before crossing. Three days later the
Israelite officers went through the camp, giving these instructions to the people: "When you see the Levitical priests
carrying the Ark of the Covenant of the Lord your God,
move out from your positions and follow them. Since you
have never traveled this way before, they will guide you.
Stay about a half mile behind them, keeping a clear distance
between you and the Ark. Make sure you don't come any
closer." Then Joshua told the people, "Purify yourselves, for
tomorrow the Lord will do great wonders among you."

Rebuilding With Old Stuff

Sometimes things happen which break our lives into pieces. It may be a relationship, the death or illness of a loved
one, our own health, economic pressures, etc. The events
cause our former lives and systems to crumble and be left

in ruins. We often don't know how to respond or even to be able to rebuild ourselves. It's a survival mentality at first and then the resolution that we will not linger in the heap of our brokenness. However, rebuilding is tricky. Sometimes we try to rebuild our lives with the materials and systems we formerly trusted and believed in. We find them inadequate and they don't fit very well. Bricks are an excellent building material for structures but when they are torn down from former buildings they are difficult to reuse. The mortar that was used is often still attached, the chipping and breaking of the bricks themselves leaves ugly scars and makes it difficult to rebuild with the old stuff. It is far easier to just start over but starting over is costly. Still, we persist in trying to rebuild with the old stuff.

It is not bad that we try. We don't know other ways to do it and the new possibilities are strange and foreboding. So we avoid them. We would much prefer to restore what was broken, what was stolen from us by simply returning to the former things. God won't allow it. It may be that the former things have been broken down because they no longer serve God's larger purpose in each of us or that they don't serve us well. In either case, we must be willing to move ahead with our lives and not be trapped by what we once knew or even trusted. The truth is we are not who we once were and so the embrace of that requires something more out of us than we may not feel we can do.

We can.

I have been on a journey back from a tragic personal loss. The experience has changed me. Sometimes I wish for the former days where life was predictable and I felt I knew who and what I was. However, there is no going back. I know that. I accept that. The door on yesterday closed with the dawn of today and though there are always memories of what once was, they are no longer part of who we are called now to be. Like the square pegs that don't fit round holes anymore, our lives require new levels of faith in God. We trust the wise master builder to provide the material that makes us who He is calling us to be.

Apparently there is something about the place you are going spiritually that is different. If you could accomplish God's plans where you are, then you would not be sensing His call to move. Yet, there is a strange uneasiness inside and you know that you cannot remain in this place. Every day you delay, you are more miserable than the day before. Get going! Embrace the courage God has given you and take the step of faith toward the future God is ordaining. Maybe it's a new job, a new relationship; a new ministry God is birthing that is part of His larger Kingdom plan. He believes in your future and has been setting you up all along for these moments . . . don't miss them!

Keep Going!

It's Coming

. . . for you are the one who will lead these people to possess all the land I swore to their ancestors I would give them. . . .[4]

The morning sunlight burst into my hotel room this morning and it awakened me far earlier than I had hoped. The comfort of my bed and the warmth of the blankets and covers made remaining in bed a wonderful and inviting thought. Yet, the longer I remained there, the more the call of the day summoned me. I began to think of things that should be done, could be done, and ought to be done. Remaining in bed was not an option. Neither is remaining in our former places, experiences or mindsets.

We sometimes make the mistake of assuming that this place—the place where we are now—is our destination. We are a people seeking comfort and security and the older we get the less likely we sometimes are to take chances or make changes that threaten our predictable lives. However, such thinking can be a trap to our future and limit our opportunity to experience what God has already arranged for us.

There is no mistaking that in moving ahead we leave behind some painful memories and we have scars to remind us of those moments we might prefer to forget. On the other hand, some of us are trapped by our former successes and we are stuck in the memories and grandeur of these to such a degree that sometimes we cannot move on! Both are deadly poison darts to our future and must not be permitted more influence than is reasonable. No matter where you are, what you are experiencing or what you may be feeling right now—I can assure you this is not the end of your journey to the happiness and fulfillment you truly desire. Such a place does exist but this is just not it!

There have been days in my recent past in which I tried to will myself to accept this present moment and not risk further injury or pain. I reasoned that if I did not take any further chance and just found a comfortable settling down place in this present moment, I would be fine. I know that is neither possible nor is it what God wants for me. I often wondered why the Children of Israel were not permitted to go to the place where Moses was buried but then I realized God knew that they might never leave that place. Graveyards are not widely known to be launching pads for future commitments.

The finality and pain of loss can create an insecurity and uncertainty about life that paralyzes the soul. No, we cannot linger long where we have hurt the most, nor can we afford to remain tethered to our past successes. The sun rises and sets each day dividing our moments that must end and new ones that must begin. It's time to get going. Perhaps you feel it is in your spirit. There is a beckoning of the Spirit that you are made for more than what is presently now. *Keep going.* . . .

We must wait for it

I overhear a young girl pleading with her father in the mall that they should wait where they were so that she can see the train that is passing through the mall with the children aboard. She hears the bell and knows it will soon be passing by where she and her father stand. The father patiently explains the train is going to be making a big circle and will be available to her wherever she is in the mall. She is not satisfied with his explanation and pleads by reasoning, "If we leave this place, we may never see the train at all!" As she waited, in time her desire was fulfilled and the train appeared. Her joy complete, her waiting rewarded.

If you follow any of my other writings, you know all too well how poorly I wait for things. It is not that I'm impatient but I'm focused and eager. When I decide its time to eat, being told that I must wait forty-five minutes for a table to begin eating is not acceptable! The same is true of getting the oil changed in my car. If that is the mission I set out to accomplish, I'm not ready to be told—leave the car and we'll call you later! However, there is value in waiting.

God told Abraham that Sarah would have a child, even at her old age, and they waited twenty-four years until the promises began to come to reality. When Isaac was born, the long years of waiting seemed but a brief moment in the view of all that was now in their hands. Later in Genesis we learn that because Jacob loved Rachel so much and was willing to work for the privilege to marry her, fourteen years did not seem a long time, even when it was part of a cruel scheme. Waiting can have enormous blessings, I suppose. It is hard though to wait, especially on God. He never seems to be in a hurry!

When God makes a promise to us, we must trust that His timing is impeccable and that the end result of our waiting will bring about more joy than we could possibly have known. There may not seem to be any joy in the waiting but the truth we know is that God is preparing for us more than we could possibly imagine!

One of the larger and continuing themes in Scripture is the process by which God promises and then requires our obedience in waiting for the promise to come to pass. Abraham was told that his descendants were going to inherit a promised land but they were going to be aliens and strangers in a foreign land for hundreds of years. Sometimes it seems odd that the promises of God given to us are not actually for us but we see them as promises, which will be for those who follow after us.

Keep in mind that man created his own devices to mark time. Time is a mystery to us. We mark time by hours, calendars, days, watches, clocks and sundials, etc. God does not. He sees the beginning and end as one and since He does, He views life, events and circumstances differently than do you and I. While we are stressing that something is not happening today, God sometimes seems silent and resolved that in time, the end result, which He already knows, will come to pass and He invites us to wait. I'm not completely clear on the issues of Divine Sovereignty and there are others who will be more gifted and spiritually attuned to help you understand but I'm coming to see more clearly that God's eternal plan for all of us will come to pass. It will be fulfilled despite all obstacles and those things which seem to throw our lives into turmoil. That should give us comfort in knowing that God keeps the world and our lives on track, never allowing anything to prevent His more perfect way. Such a God who can be trusted to manage the issues and matters of our lives is worthy of our most faithful lives!

We must battle to get there

The Jordan River was a place of transition for the moving group of people who were descendants of that multitude which came out of Egypt on the fateful night that every firstborn of man and beast were stricken by the death angel in the final act of God's judgment on Pharaoh and his hardened heart. Moses and the Israelites came out of Egypt as slaves and spent forty years moving through a wilderness experience. Through disobedience and stubbornness most of them did not complete the journey. Instead, God's judgment fell on them and they were buried in the hot sands of the Sinai desert.

It was their children and grandchildren who eventually came to move into the land God had promised and even at that, there was an understanding that God would require them to possess the land. Make no mistake, God's promise was sure—they would live in the land—but they would have to fight to possess it. God did not drive out the inhabitants and as the narrative would show, there were years of battles and struggle until all the enemies had been conquered. The same is true of our lives. God's promises to us are true and genuine. I firmly believe that every promise God makes is true and we will gain all but the future may require our strongest efforts against the enemy who seeks to steal our hope and faith in God's promises.

I wish life were easier than it is. In fact, I wish that we could know life without sorrow or pain. How differently we might live in this earth, if there were no sin, no sickness or death. I know in my own life that sometimes I imagine what life would be like if such an existence here on earth were possible. However, it is not. When I think about that, I realize that what we are describing is heaven—and it is life as God intended it to be. It is but one of the things that makes our eternal future so amazing and so desirable.

So how will we get there? It will sometimes be a struggle and you will have to battle against your feelings, emotions and experiences. We cannot escape the battle that is between our destiny and us. It is the plan of God that we press on, fighting the necessary good fight of faith and laying hold of the promises God has designed for our lives.

There was the man who walked into my office one day seeking my advice and counsel about how to leverage his past into a ministry future that would enable him to embrace what God had planned. The problem was John's past was filled with many hurdles to overcome—decisions he made and judgments by others that by all intents seemed insurmountable. So he walked humbly, believing God had spoken and called him. As authorities began to explore the pieces of his past broken life they found none of the things he feared they would. Strangely, certain segments of time were inexplicably invisible, or so it seemed, to those who had the authority to limit his possibilities. When it was done and the doors of opportunity flew wide open, John was amazed and in his heart he heard the whisper of God *"he whom the Son sets free is free indeed!"* In fact, it is the name of his ministry—FREE INDEED. I don't know what happened. I don't know how God did it, but He did. He ordained a future for John that was His plan and God did not allow even his difficult past to prevent it from coming. The enemy cannot stop John. Neither can his past. What God has determined is greater than his past or his present. As he continues to put his trust in the Lord, he is finding that God's grace and power is at work—writing new chapters for his life and enabling him to transcend his past. Every time I think of him, I smile knowing the decision he has made to refuse the pull of what once defined him and determined to embrace what God has chosen to bring to pass!

The promises of God were so sure and the future of God so ordained that no enemy in their path could prevent the Children of Israel from possession of the land. The same is true for you and me. Our lives belong to God and when we commit our whole hearts to Him, He ensures our journey to the purposes and peace of God. You may feel you are prevented from living beyond the past or the struggles of all that you have experienced but know this. God is bigger. He is bigger than your obstacles. His plans are bigger than your fears. There is another day coming for you.

Anticipate that and ***Keep Going***!

No Going Back

*Wherever you set foot, you will be
on land I have given you. . . .*[5]

5   Joshua 1:4 NLT

One of the fascinating stories of Scripture is the Old Testament narrative of Ruth, the Moabite and her mother-in-law, Naomi. From the story, we learn that Naomi and her family have moved from their home in Bethlehem to Moab during a time of famine and while there Naomi saw the death of her husband and two sons. After she's buried them all, she makes a difficult decision and finally begins the long journey to return home to Bethlehem. It is an emotional journey because she and her family had come to Moab with such high hopes and expectations and she is now living without the people who first walked the journey with her. So much of who she is and what she dreamed about is being left in Moab and going home, while the sensible choice, is not the exciting return she may have once thought it might be.

She has two daughters-in-law with her as the journey begins until Naomi stops and offers both of them the chance to return and find new husbands. One of the women, Orpah, does return to her family and leaves, but the other, Ruth, decides to remain with Naomi and trust her future to the faith and God of Naomi. In time, Ruth finds love in a man named Boaz who is a kinsman redeemer to her according to the Biblical customs and together they have a son named Obed, who is in the lineage of Jesus Christ. It is a fascinating story of hope, faith and courage.

I'm drawn to the strong decision of Ruth to remain with Naomi, despite the fact there is no other son for Ruth to marry and no hope that her future will get any better. Yet, she courageously chooses to stay and be part of Naomi's life story. We would need to appreciate in greater detail the issues of Jewish custom to know that back in Bethlehem,

Ruth has no social standing, no security and no hope of finding it with Naomi, who is now an aged widow. It is one of life's ultimate "throw caution to the wind" moments and this young woman does so because there is something in Naomi that inspires her and as Ruth scans the landscape of the future, there is nothing to go back to in her former life. Yet in Naomi, there is a hope and while I cannot specifically trace the points, I find the faith of her hope for the future in the following words, which are dramatically spoken and often repeated. Perhaps they will inspire you again as they often do me. . . .

> . . . and Orpah kissed her mother-in-law good-bye. But Ruth clung tightly to Naomi. "Look," Naomi said to her, "your sister-in-law has gone back to her people and to her gods. You should do the same." But Ruth replied, "Don't ask me to leave you and turn back. Wherever you go, I will go; wherever you live, I will live. Your people will be my people, and your God will be my God. Wherever you die, I will die, and there I will be buried. May the Lord punish me severely if I allow anything but death to separate us!" When Naomi saw that Ruth was determined to go with her, she said nothing more.[6]

According to custom and law, Ruth was not free to marry anyone she wanted but had to marry someone in her husband's family line and since she was not a Jew by birth, but a Gentile, the likelihood that would occur was not high. Additionally, Ruth is a widow and dealing with her own grief and adjustment to life without the one person she had previously pledged her heart to.

Ruth's resolve moves me. She is choosing life at risk, in a strange new land with new customs, a new God and new relationships. She is opting, out of love for Naomi, to cast aside her own wishes and dreams to be near to and assist

---

6 Ruth 1:14b-18 NLT

this woman whose life has been decimated by three close family deaths. She adamantly tells Naomi—I'm not going back!

Pastor Sheryl Brady addresses this in her book, *You've Got It In You.* . . .

> Whether you're familiar with Ruth's story or not, I believe we all know how scary it can be to move from one place to another. It's not just exchanging the familiar for the unknown; moving forces us to look within ourselves and find more strength than we knew we had, more courage than we've ever displayed before, and more faith in the goodness of our loving Father than we've ever had to show. Sometimes we have to move in order to survive. Even when it's too risky, it's still tempting to stay where we are. You don't have to take the promotion; you can just stay with the position you have and the job security that it provides. If you go up the ladder at work, there's always a chance you could fall even further if you fail. But can you live with the questions that will forever gnaw at your peace? The questions that will creep into your mind at the end of the day as you're attempting to sleep: I wonder if I would have been even more successful if I'd taken that job? I wonder if our family would've been happier if we'd moved? What if God had something special for me in that new place that I was too afraid to take hold of? What if I've missed a blessing by being blinded by my fears? Each of us has a choice every day either to remain in the Moab of our lives, the place with people just like us, the place where we've always belonged, the place that makes no real demands on us, or to embark on a journey of faith into a new country. Naomi was compelled to return to her homeland because of the dire circumstances she experienced in Moab, but her daughter-in-law Ruth clearly had a choice.[7]

The Long Overdue Goodbye. . . .

On a dark winter night at the conclusion of a family holiday season, my sons and their wives packed up the cars and said their goodbyes to me. I hugged my one grandson, at the

7   Sheryl Brady, *You've Got It In You*, Howard Books. New York. NY. 2012. Pages 3-4

time, holding him tightly and made sure the car seat was in place and watched as my children pulled away heading back to their own homes. I wept like a baby. In fact, I was so emotional as they pulled away that they called back in a few minutes offering to return home in case I needed them to. There was no need and their return would have only meant another dreadful and teary goodbye. I hate goodbyes and yet there is no escaping them. It seems they are just part of the landscape of our lives, one of those things in life that we just have to accept. Sometimes our separations are short and temporary and others are more final and lasting. Each of us has stood in a cold graveyard and realized that our good-byes were more impacting than others. Maybe that is why heaven will be such a special place where there will never be a goodbye.

There are some goodbyes that we need! In some cases, we all need a good parting and the decision to end something that no longer defines and advances and our life assignments. It is true that we often hold on too long to things that we should have stopped long before. However, saying goodbye to things, relationships and places that are rich with loving and positive memories is never easy. A child does not want to give up the broken toy because it brings a strange but wonderful comfort. I have a friend who held on to a cell phone she no longer uses because it has sentimental value and pleasant memories. We all have things like that . . . a symbol that marks another time in life when we remember fondly. There is nothing wrong with retaining some things as long as they don't prevent us from the movement forward that God calls for.

The problem arises when we refuse to let go of things that limit us and keep us from the plans God has. Jacob, because

of his insecurity and the impact of all the losses he has experienced with the death of Rachel, his wife and Joseph,
his son (whom he thinks is dead, although we know he is
not!) is a prime example of this point. He refuses to allow
his youngest and last remaining son with Rachel, Benjamin,
to go with the other sons back to Egypt at the order of the
man there who holds the key to the food they will need to
keep their families alive. He does not know that it is the son
he thought was lost, his beloved Joseph who has given the
order! Nor does he have a clue that this piece of the journey
is part of God's plan to rescue Jacob and his family. All Jacob knows is that letting go is hard and he cannot do it until
the reality of his own demise is so imminent that he has no
alternative but to let go of Benjamin. When he finally does
decide that Benjamin can go, his words of resignation are
noteworthy. . . .

> Their father *(Jacob)* gave in. "If it has to be, it has to be. But
> do this: stuff your packs with the finest products from the land
> you can find and take them to the man as gifts—some balm and
> honey, some spices and perfumes, some pistachios and almonds.
> And take plenty of money—pay back double what was returned
> to your sacks; that might have been a mistake. Take your brother
> *(Benjamin)* and get going. Go back to the man. And may The
> Strong God give you grace in that man's eyes so that he'll send
> back your other brother along with Benjamin. For me, nothing's
> left; I've lost everything."[8]

What happens next is mind-boggling! In the letting go of
Benjamin, God unlocks for Jacob, for his sons and family
and for a nation, the amazing plan of God to bring about
restoration, healing and a future. If Jacob simply refuses
to let go and stubbornly insists that Benjamin will not go,
what happens to Jacob, his family and the future God has
ordained?

8 Genesis 43:11-14 The Message (emphasis mine)

You may wonder why God did not let the Children of Israel climb up Mount Nebo with Moses and say their farewells and bury him there. It may be that God knew they would never leave that place and in remaining there, they would never go to where their destiny summoned them. I know that temptation. The lure of remaining in places of comfort and security can be strong and we all have battled the temptation to just stay where we are and never go further. However, that is not our future. We are not made to remain in this place or this moment forever. This is just a place in our lives now but our future lies ahead and in moving forward, we make the commitment to say goodbye to this place and look forward to the next moments God has ordained.

I sometimes wonder why life has such decisive moments. As you think back, you can probably point to a few in your life where a critical decision to move, to believe, to hope beyond the present moment, changed the trajectory of your life. These divine intersections are so valuable to the life God is calling us to live. Without them, we would be merely going through the motions and never embracing the potential of a future that could change the world for the kingdom.

If Ruth goes back with her sister-in-law, Orpah, what becomes of her? She never meets Boaz, she never sees the transforming of Naomi's life and she certainly does not become a mother in the birth order of Jesus Christ. That single decision to remain with Naomi changed everything for Ruth and for others, including me. As we leave this chapter and go on, I leave you with the following words scripted by someone else who is imagining the kind of dialogue that could have taken place between Ruth and Naomi that defining day in both women's life. . . .

"Ms. Naomi, I can't go back. I have nothing to go back for. Things are different now. Knowing you has changed my life. I was incomplete without you. I found God in you and from there I found purpose. Yes, Ms. Naomi, you were the one who connected me to my destiny! You told me who I was. You told me what I could become. You woke up the sleeping things that were inside of me. I'm awake now and it's all because of you! How in the world do you think I could go back to sleep now? Whatever I've got to do, I'll do it. Whatever I've got to change, I'll change it, but you can't leave me where I am! My heart is fixed. "Wherever you go, I'm going. Wherever you live is where I'm living. And whenever we've walked together as far as we can walk, wherever you die is where I want to die. And wherever they lay you down, I want them to leave a spot for me right there beside you! "Ms. Naomi, I don't know where we are going and, to be honest, it really doesn't matter. If we are starting over, then guess what? We are doing it together!"[9]

We were never called to go back. Yesterday is in the rearview mirror and the approaching lights of tomorrow beckon us to believe for all that God is doing and calling for in us.

Keep Going!

9 Sheryl Brady, *You've Got It In You*. Howard Books. New York, NY. Page 11-12

STUCK

For I will be with you as I was with Moses. I will not fail you or abandon you. "Be strong and courageous, for you are the one who will lead these people to possess all the land I swore to their ancestors I would give them."[10]

---
10 Joshua 1:5 NLT

If you are like me, sometimes life can feel like you are on an interstate highway and there is a jam of traffic that stretches for miles and miles and you poke along, not knowing what is holding up traffic. You start switching lanes, at every opportunity, to try and get moving but as soon as you leave one lane for another, your former lane starts moving quicker and you regret your decision. The stopping and starting leaves you exhausted, frazzled and frustrated at the lack of progress. Depending on how far back you are, often by the time the traffic clears up and is moving again and you get to the point that caused the snarl, everything is cleaned up and you have no idea why you have been languishing at a snail's pace for the past hour!

When life seems stuck, you are forced to make some decisions. Either you can remain in the position you are—or you make the choice to get moving again! The children of Israel must have felt like they were stuck when they left Egypt and instead of a journey of a few days, they spent forty years wandering in the wilderness. Look at a map and follow them as they circle around and around the same landscapes and land markers. Logistically, it should only have taken them a short time to make the journey but in reality it lasted forty years! *Why did God allow them to make so little progress in pursuit of His promise to bring them to land? Why was the process so slow and unproductive from the standpoint of the people?* They were often bored and in their boredom, they made serious personal and moral mistakes, often because they failed to appreciate the process God had them in.

Here's an important verse of Scripture that explains some of the reasoning God had. . . .

> And you shall remember that the Lord your God led you all the
> way these forty years in the wilderness, to humble you and test

you, to know what was in your heart, whether you would keep
His commandments or not. So He humbled you, allowed you to
hunger, and fed you with manna which you did not know nor
did your fathers know, that He might make you know that man
shall not live by bread alone; but man lives by every word that
proceeds from the mouth of the Lord.[11]

It is clear to me that God wanted Pharaoh to follow them
out into the desert so He could forever destroy the enemy
who threatened to bring them back to Egypt. It is also apparent that God had a plan that was not clear to the traveling Israelites. In the same way, your life may have taken
some turns that appear to leave you bewildered and unsure
of how to proceed. *You may wonder if God is not close or
is He no longer guiding you?* You would not be the first to
feel that way. Thousands of years before you had that question, the Israelites wondered—*Why did God bring us out
here to die?* Of course He did not bring them out to die and
only those who disobeyed or acted without regard to God's
instruction died but they did have questions that sometimes
led to decisions that were not helpful in their journey.

In the aftermath of tragic moments, it may feel like the
world has shifted on its axis and there is much that looks
very unfamiliar. You feel like you got off at the wrong stop
and instead of seeing the landmarks of your former life, you
see new ones and they can make you afraid. I know that
feeling. So do many others who have navigated the significant changes that life can bring to you. What I'm learning
is that life is not predictable and even the most spiritual of
us can find the shifts in life that come to threaten our peace
and when those thoughts linger, there is a distinct possibil-
ity that we will get stuck between where we have been and
where we are to go.

11 Deuteronomy 8:2-3 NLT

It is in such moments that movement is slow and many times even non-existent, in part because life has captured your confidence and you no longer have the security of knowing what to expect or how to proceed. Your old systems no longer work and even when you attempt to rebuild your life it feels awkward, like something is missing. When times got tough, notice how favorable it appeared to feel to the Children of Israel to return to Egypt. *Did they want to return to slavery?* Of course not. What they wanted was the security of their former lives and if they had to accept slavery to do that, they would! I know that sounds strange but few of us thrive in settings and environments that are constantly changing. We crave security and happiness in our lives and when we don't have it, we are miserable.

For some time now, I've been attempting to learn what is in my heart and one of my startling discoveries was how much I crave happiness. Because these recent days have been so filled with sadness, I think my appetite for happiness has been even more than I thought. The problem is I cannot create my own happiness. In fact, the more I try to create happiness the more elusive it seems to be. Happiness only seems to come when my heart is aligned to God and His purposes for my life. When I do that, happiness seems more attainable to me. What was even more startling to me is how much I was willing to do to be happy—to attempt to make myself happy or in some ways convince myself that I was happy! Of course, like Solomon, in time, I became exhausted in my futile attempts to manufacture happiness. Solomon writes, *"So I came to hate life because everything done here under the sun is so troubling. Everything is meaningless—like chasing the wind."*[12] So it is with all who seek

12 Ecclesiastes 2:17 NLT

to find happiness in anything else but the Creator whose love and attention to us is so pure. Remember, He said, *"I know what I'm doing. I have it all planned out—plans to take care of you, not abandon you, plans to give you the future you hope for."*[13]

I don't know how to tell you this in a way that makes it easier to swallow, but there is no returning to the former path. It ended when the moments came that altered life as you know it. Maybe it was the reorganization of the factory or the aftermath of a bitter betrayal of your spouse and the impending divorce. Perhaps it is the shock of grief that came when your loved one passed away and you feel helpless to know how you are supposed to proceed. In all of these and dozens of others, the feeling that you are stuck is overwhelming and while you know you need to move, movement is neither easy nor comfortable. So we wait but in waiting we are again watching others move on while we feel trapped in the vortex of our own emotions, feelings and hopelessness. You may feel cheated or that God has not dealt fairly with you in these kinds of things and those feelings are not wrong, in my opinion—just don't linger there too long!

I wish God always answered us in timely fashion. I wish there was a 100% predictability factor on prayer and other decision-making moments when we need them. However, some people pray a lifetime and God never changes the circumstances. However, He does change us, if we are ready to keep going and see what He will do! Some of the best people in God's family get stuck and they don't know what to do. *What is the proper response to the crisis you just encountered, or how should you reorganize your life around a new normal that feels awkward and unnerving?* Again, the

---

13   Jeremiah 29:11 Message

shift in your life is obvious but the steps ahead are not always as clear as we wish. It is in these moments we discover for ourselves if faith works. Those moments when you could not understand, you had no back-up plan and yet your heart kept telling you to trust and believe in God. It is raw and simple faith that gets your through. The fundamental hope that we have in God, that He is true and faithful and when our life is stuck, He is not. He is not worried or fretting over the things I am. He is not concerned that time is passing and I don't know how to proceed. He calls me to wait and know that when it is right, my movement will come.

I think about my friend Joseph, (we don't actually know each other literally but I've written and preached enough to call him "friend" . . .) who at the age of seventeen dreamed about a day when his brothers would come and bow down to him. He was a dreamy and lofty young man who seems to brag about this destiny moment. However, follow his timeline and it is filled with moments when his life feels stuck in neutral and there is absolutely no movement toward destiny. He is betrayed and sold by his brothers to flesh peddlers who make a buck on the man who will one day be the second most powerful man on the planet. He just did not know how or when. He is tempted by his boss' wife to commit sexual sins and in refusing he is sent by his well-placed employer to jail and further away from the potential reality of his dreams. He feels he is wasting time and precious years of potential waiting on other criminals and making sure they get their dreams interpreted and daily care as a trustee and I'm sure he wondered the same question you and I wonder in the quiet moments of life after we try to pick up the pieces of our former brokenness.

When is it my turn?

My grandsons often use their mother's phone to play games and watch movies. I've witnessed first hand their frustration at one another while they wait for one or the other to finish and share. From time to time, someone has to answer the question, *when is it my turn?* Jarius is a man of influence and authority but he has a problem with his little girl. She is very sick and without help, she may die. So he leaves his home one day in search of a man whom he has been told could, if he chose to, heal his daughter and make her well without another visit to the doctor. He finds Jesus and implores him to come to his house and touch the sick girl. Jesus agrees but as they travel, someone else steps into Jarius' story and her miracle occurs during the transit to Jarius' house. Instead of getting Jesus there in time, while he is waiting on this other woman's story to finish, he gets word that the girl has died and there is no need to complete the mission he started his day with. In his own mind, his daughter is dead and from there, the rest is not important. If she is dead, then everything is changed. Life priorities and plans for the future are lost or relegated to the 'what does it matter now' pile of discarded hopes and dreams. As he processes his frustration and doubts (and he has them), Jesus turns to him and says, *"Only believe"*[14]

What does that mean, really? I wish I truly knew. I used to think I did but then at a critical time from my point of view, faith did not work as I supposed and my hope was lost and buried in a coffin that sits right now in a cemetery that feels to me like the place where dreams go to die. However, I'm reshaping my concepts of faith and finding that faith is not the magic pill that fulfills all my wishes and hopes. Rather,

---

14 Mark 5:36 NASB

faith is an abiding confidence in who God is—not what He does. Job responds like this *"though He slay me, still I will trust him."*[15] I'm getting there and in time, I believe I will see again the faith that transcends doubts brought by painful moments that cannot be wished away or made to cease just because I want them to or ask Him to remove them.

Stop Thinking and Start Living

I remember sitting in the food court of my local mall one evening, watching people going by and wondering if any of them cared what was happening to me. In moments, I began to feel the impulse that my thinking was too inward and to self-focused. The more I sat there, the more I tried to think through my problems, my emotions, my feelings and in time I was totally depressed in my spirit. I realized that so much of my energy was being spent on thinking, analyzing, questioning that I had stopped living. Instead of rising each day with a passion to live for the Lord, I was focusing my energy on seeking to outthink God—to analyze Him at some level that would enable me to understand things that are too high for me to know. It was a releasing moment when I started out of that mall, asking God to restore my desires to live, to embrace the future and know that despite what I did not know, what I could to change, I was alive and in living, there is hope! *Can you do business with a God who holds all the cards and only moves when He wants to and only does what He chooses to do?* We have to because there is no other option except to give up on life and refuse to move forward. I don't plan to live that way. I'm trusting that I'm able to again choose life and the return of the hope that once beat so strongly in my heart.

---

15 Job 13:15 NKJV

There are those who don't allow for believers to doubt or have questions about God. If you're one of those persons, then don't let me offend you or discount your strong and abiding faith. I do believe and yet like the father of a demon-controlled son in Mark 8, I ask God to help my unbelief and accept that His grace is enough for my journey, one day at a time. The journey beyond this moment here is in the willingness to take the next step. No matter how hard it may seem, the next step to release your faith toward the future may very well open up the rest of your life.

Embrace it and *Keep Going*!

DIRECTION

"This is my command—be strong and courageous! Do not be afraid or discouraged. For the Lord your God is with you wherever you go."[16] (Emphasis mine)

---

16 Joshua 1:9 NLT

This instruction from God to Joshua is among my favorite verses in the Scriptures. How many times have I gone there to find the confidence to press ahead with decisions and issues that cause me to fear or be intimidated? I can relate to Joshua. He has been given a seemingly impossible human task to take a significant group of people to the reality of God's full and complete promise to give them possession of land that He swore to Abraham and his descendants. However, the promise must be gained and possessed and that requires a leader who can navigate the moments, lead decisively and make sound decisions, all of that in an environment of people who have been wandering for forty years in pursuit of this dream. His followers are not afraid to challenge leadership and there will be a good share of cynical people who have seen it all when Moses was the leader. So Joshua has his work cut out for him.

Yet, God calmly and confidently says, *"I'm with you, no matter what!"* and strongly reminds Joshua of his earlier command to be *"strong and very courageous"*. In fact, if you go back to the beginning of the chapter, you will find that God gives Joshua that command in various forms, four times! Why such an emphasis on courage? Perhaps it is because God knows us better than we know ourselves. He knows in the face of opposition, discouragement and unexpected turns in the road we will become afraid, sometimes to the point of quitting.

Perhaps you can relate. You once stood on the power of a strong promise God made and yet the circumstances or environments of your present state look nothing like you thought. In fact, you may feel you are further from the realization of your dreams than when you started! One of the mysterious things about God is that He does not always show His full hand to us. God is engaged in processes and events around us that we don't yet see and in the right time, He will unfold the next steps in ways that cause us to shake our heads because we cannot see it in advance.

Return with me to the story of Joseph and his transition from a dream of destiny and purpose to the unjust imprisonment because someone lied about his intentions and actions. While in that jail, it may have seemed that Joseph's life was off track and his dreams derailed but that would be a mistake to assume because as we see the story unfold, Joseph was precisely in the position God planned and needed for the fulfillment of a divine plan. If Joseph is not in that prison, he never meets the wine taster who eventually tells Pharaoh about Joseph and it is Joseph who reveals the dreams that God gave Pharaoh to preserve both the land and Joseph and his family. He does not see it at the time, but he continues to believe and later he says to his brothers,

> And he said again, "I am Joseph, your brother, whom you sold into slavery in Egypt. But don't be upset, and don't be angry with yourselves for selling me to this place. **It was God who sent me here ahead of you to preserve your lives.**[17] (Emphasis mine)

Maybe you think that the promotion you were passed over was a bad thing for you. Just remember this, when our ways are pleasing to the Lord and we commit ourselves to Him, we can know for sure that He is at work in the details of life at levels that are significantly important but largely unknown to us until the time God chooses to unveil His plans. That's why trust is so valued by our God and so vital to our relationship to God. We trust that He sees and knows what we don't and that when the time comes, He will write the script for the next chapter of our lives, bringing us to the

---

17 Genesis 45:4-5 NLT

place of divine fulfillment. When it comes, we know it was God who pulled it off and not ourselves.

It is in this area where the enemy does so much damage to our confidence and his tricks are not new. He is a deceiver and he tries to convince us that God is not trustworthy and that we must take matters into our own hands, lest we fail to achieve our goals. Yet, we are called to be obedient and faithful, not to rule the universe and arrange our futures. The Lord orders our steps and the Psalmist declares, *"He establishes them . . ."*[18] If He does, then He knows the way we should go, when we should move and how. It should remove all the pressure from life. Because it doesn't, we are tempted to doubt and fear and God knows that about Joshua and He knows that about me. Believe me, I know fear and it has a crippling effect on the confidence of a leader. However, this passage and others are reminders that God knows my fears and challenges me to believe in Him and have full confidence in His ability and not my own.

Where are you headed?

I'm confident that every person on the earth has a God assignment. It is the reason you are still here on the earth. When that assignment is completed, then your life on this earth will end. I believe so strongly in that principle that I feel it is imperative that you seek God and enlist the help of others to find your mission in life and begin living it out immediately. First, because it only makes sense to be aligned to God's purposes as early in life as you can. Secondly, God is expecting you to do what He has placed you here on the earth to do. Finding that out and charting the course is an important piece of the *Keep Going* philosophy of life.

18 Psalms 40:2 NJKV

It has been my experience through the years that many good and faithful people struggle to connect their everyday lives to purposes and objectives that have God's imprint on them. They either don't realize their divine potential or have a spiritual block to obtain their purpose. In some cases, it may be fear or intimidation and in others, it may simply be ignorance of the principle. Still others resist because they don't want to do what God has commanded them to do. Jonah was such an individual called by God and given a specific assignment for his life. However, that was not something Jonah was comfortable doing and so he chose another path. It was the first of several missteps and misapplied logic that eventually put him into the belly of a great fish. Don't be misled; God's will is going to be done upon the earth. Accept that fact and begin embracing your place in God's plan. There is great joy in knowing that you are doing what God has commanded you to do. Don't shy away or feel that you are not capable because God never calls you to assignments that you are incapable of doing. He knows you so well and in His knowledge, He has designed a purpose that enables you to succeed at what you do. Resisting God's plan is disobedience and only positions us for greater frustration in life.

When sincere seekers of God ask how to find His will for life, I have a simple two-question inquiry.

What are you passionate about?
What are you gifted to do?

If you understand the answer to those two questions you will find, in my opinion, a good starting point for what God is asking you to do with your life. I strongly disagree that God is calling you to assignments for which you have no passion and no ability. Rather, I think God uses our innate passion for particular things and then couples that with the talent and gifting that have always been part of who we are. Take for example, a person who has a passion for creativity and reflection. They scribble and draw on almost everything and imagine designs that are beautiful and inspire. It is not likely that person is called to be an accountant in life! On the other hand, if a person cannot sing and has no musical ability or even if they have desire to do so, it is not likely that God is calling them to a public singing ministry! Now, you and I both know people like that whose desire for some vocation did not line up with their talents and it was both sad and funny to witness. Buck Owens of the TV show, *Hee Haw* was the only person I knew who made a decent living singing without any real ability to do so! (for younger readers, you may need to check with your parents or some older person to know who I'm talking about).

God is smarter than we are and He knows how to position us in places where our obedience and faithfulness coupled with His mighty power brings a victory that advances God's plan for the world. It is what we all want to do with our lives and so it is vital that we know what God is calling us to do and begin working for Him. Think about someone who wastes their entire life doing things that are not in alignment with God's plans and how much they have missed? I don't want to do that with my life and I have chosen despite the challenges of my life, I'm going to serve the Lord with faithfulness and do my best to complete the assignment for which I was born upon the earth.

You may think that is all well and good for someone like me but your life has been shattered by the pain or disappointment of events and/or people in such magnitude that there is simply no energy to go on! Let me carefully say that

God's grace is big enough and His mercy to you is enough to get through whatever you face. How? One step, one moment at a time. Take the next moment and commit it to God, trusting Him to make it what it should be and you will find He puts together the most difficult of issues for purposes that are larger and bigger than you are!

Gideon was a man who lived in relative obscurity, never assuming that he would ever do anything mighty for God. He lived in a time when enemies of his country were constantly ravaging the crops and decimating the land. Gideon's family and relatives were constantly surviving the attacks day after day. Then one day, an angel of God shows up and tells Gideon that God has chosen him to be the leader of a plan God has for deliverance to the people of God. Gideon is stunned and humbly reminds God that he is the most unlikely of all people to be used for such an important task. Notice the language. . . .

> But Lord," Gideon replied, "How can I rescue Israel? My clan is the weakest in the whole tribe of Manasseh, and I am the least in my entire family!"[19]

Gideon is not a confident soul. Yet, God used him and a great victory was won. The key to the victory was not Gideon's ability but his willingness and obedience to God's command. The power that brings the victory belongs to the Lord. We are merely His hands and feet through which He works. If it were up to us, then our ability would be the critical point. It's not and thankfully so. Therefore, the power is God's and He chooses to manifest it through our lives and obedient hearts. He did with Gideon and He does with you.

19 Judges 6:15 NLT

What if God is with us?

We might wish that life were more predictable and that we could guarantee our success in moments when great trust is required. I know from my own life there will always be moments when the uncertainty of life challenges our faith and we are tempted to pull back our forward motion. We fear not being adequate or that we will fail and so we hold back, unsure of the outcome. Isn't that what faith is about? By faith, we trust in what we cannot see or touch, believing that God is doing what we cannot do. By trusting in Him, we put all of our hopes in One who has proven to us over and over that He can be trusted always.

So how differently do we live going forward, if we truly believed God was with us? I know in saying that some are quick to respond—of course, we know God is with us—but the truth is we don't often live that way. We are like the disciples in Luke 8 who have Jesus in the boat with them and they still fear they will not survive the storm! That's why He rebuked them for their lack of faith. If they could not believe for the security with the Creator of the universe in the boat with them, then when do we believe in His protecting grace over our lives?

I wish I could boast that my faith is always strong but that would not be true. More times than I would want to confess, my faith is much like the disciples in this boat. I'm pleading with God for safety, security, provision, or whatever and failing to appreciate that He is with me, right there, engaged in the battles of my daily life. We are not alone . . . ever!

In the dark of my soul and when I cannot seem to make heads or tails of the road I'm to take, there is a confidence that comes from a promise that He made and it remains a constant reminder to those of us who tend to worry too much. As we close this chapter, read it slowly and then close your eyes and ask yourself the question—*what changes about where I am or where I am going, if in fact, the Lord is with me?* Right now, I believe that peace will wash over your soul like you have not felt in many days. Go ahead . . . it's time. Your peace has come!

> For He Himself has said, "I will never leave you nor forsake you." So we may boldly say: The Lord *is* my helper; I will not fear. What can man do to me?[20]

Keep Going!

---

20 Hebrews 13:5-6 NKJV

STICKY

Then the Lord said to Joshua, "Today I have rolled away the shame of your slavery in Egypt." So that place has been called Gilgal to this day.

Teflon or polytetrafluoroethylene was discovered on April 6, 1938 by Dr. Roy Plunkett at the DuPont research laboratories (Jackson Laboratory in New Jersey). Plunkett was working with gases related to Freon refrigerants when upon checking a frozen, compressed sample of tetrafluoroethylene, he and his associates discovered that the sample had polymerized spontaneously into a white, waxy solid to form polytetrafluoroethylene or PTFE. The surface is so slippery; virtually nothing sticks to it or is absorbed by it.[21]

My mother had some cooking vessels with this finish and I recall that fried foods would not stick and she cleaned them with a simple wipe of a damp cloth. I've been thinking that maybe we need Teflon on our spirits. Perhaps we should allow God to prepare our hearts in ways that simply refuses to allow the words or deeds of others or even our own actions to stick to us. Those things that happen to us can sometimes attach themselves and change the perception we have of our futures and ourselves. Such things can even crush the hope God intends for our lives. What if we refused to be defined by what used to be and instead accepted ourselves as God has chosen to see us—free, whole and redeemed?

Unless you have been there, you cannot appreciate how difficult it is to get rid of a bad reputation. Something that marked your life years ago and no one seems to forget and no matter how much you do, you are always labeled with the reminder of what or who you once were. People can be cruel in this respect and sometimes a first impression can be impossible to shake.

Take Gretchen (not her real name), a young woman with whom I became acquainted some time ago. She possessed a beau-

21 http://inventors.about.com/library/inventors/blteflon.htm

tiful personality and all the intangibles that made her very popular in her school and church. She was a leader and it was clear to all of us that she was potentially on a career and ministry track that was exciting to consider. What a future or so it seemed, until the night she made a fateful decision that changed everything. Now her amazing little son reminds me of my own sons and I always get joy in seeing the pictures of he and his mommy as they grow together. Life has changed for my young friend and one of the hardest things is how people struggle to handle her now. Is she still the high potential young leader in the making or is she the girl of her decisions? She is both. Gretchen is still amazing and her courage in raising a son and trying to move forward with her life inspires many others and me. Here's hoping Gretchen stays focused on the future and refuses to allow the judgment of others to stick to her.

It's the stickiness of these assessments others make of our lives that can sometimes make a difference for us. A parent makes a statement in frustration that attaches itself to a child who never seems to find the inner confidence that they are good enough for the demanding parent. A co-worker criticizes and you spend a lifetime trying to live out beyond their words. There once was a guy in my life named Mike who was never has been able to shake the words of his father that he was not highly motivated enough to be a success in life. So after failed marriages and many career resets, he still overworks himself to prove his father wrong. The only problem is that his father has been dead for years. Unfortunately, Mike is unable to shake the stickiness of his dead father's words.

The power of the words from others can be devastating to the commitments to keep going with your life. Often you have to disengage the things that attach themselves to you before you can move on but it is not easy. How we view ourselves and how much we allow the view of others to influence has a great deal to do with how successful we will be in the progress of our life journey.

Joshua and the people who are traveling with him are former slaves in Egypt but they are now on the way to a new destiny and in the new land. They are no longer slaves and yet they often acted like slaves, talked and thought like slaves. What a challenge for these people because the people of Egypt may see them as former slaves but God does not. In a classic passage, God whispers to Joshua just before they conquer Jericho

> Then the Lord said to Joshua, "Today I have rolled away the reproach of Egypt from you." So the name of that place is called Gilgal to this day.[22]

The word from the Lord signals that the scourge of their former lives was wiped away by the act of God Himself. What a powerful announcement that God was supernaturally removing those former tags and putting them into a new light as they step into this new life in Canaan! Maybe in the secret places of your life you are wishing that God would do that for you—wipe away the reproaches that have marked you for a lifetime. Here is the secret God has wanted you to know all along. He already has wiped the slate clean.

Do you need that? Are you weighted with things that have stuck to your life and have been obstacles to the kind of obedience and surrender God is calling for in you? You would not be the first human being to struggle here. On some level, we all do. Our human tendency is to believe the worst and to accept as truth what the enemy means to hold us back. In

---

22 Joshua 5:9 NASB

Christ, we are free from the former lives we lived and we are free to pursue life as God intends it. Our enemies cannot hold us back. Our past cannot define our future, unless we allow it. In the power of our God, we are free from the weights that hold us.

> Therefore, since we are surrounded by such a huge crowd of witnesses to the life of faith, let us strip off every weight that slows us down, especially the sin that so easily trips us up. And let us run with endurance the race God has set before us.[23]

My family, has at times, enjoyed the sitcom *Everybody Loves Raymond*. There is one particular episode that exemplifies what I'm trying to convey to you. In this particular episode, Raymond's brother is getting married to Amy and during the ceremony his mother interrupts and creates a very uncomfortable environment for the entire wedding party and guests. The carryover dampens the mood in the reception party and Raymond is left to offer a toast to his brother and new bride. In his attempt to put a positive spin on the entire bizarre event, he reminds his brother and the wedding guests how the use of "editing" has been his family's way of erasing the painful memories and only remembering the good ones. Raymond offers that only the good memories remain and the painful ones are simply edited away. It is a humorous reminder of a great principle that in Christ, God has edited out the bad places of our former selves and given us a new life that is formed in the image of Himself.

I don't know how God does it but He does. By His power, He brings our minds to places where we remember the things that make for our future and the words, memories or former acts of our past that once caused us such pain are

---

23 Hebrews 12:1 NLT

rendered powerless. There is a hope that those who once sought to hurt us . . . cannot . . . and the things we thought would surely destroy us . . . cannot! It is these words from a well-worn verse that inspire me to realize this. See if you can see what I mean. . . .

> But in that coming day no weapon turned against you will succeed. You will silence every voice raised up to accuse you. These benefits are enjoyed by the servants of the LORD; their vindication will come from me. I, the LORD, have spoken![24]

There are some old paths you cannot go back down again.

We are sometimes tempted to return to old places where there is the comfort of what once was. Our memories seem to draw us back and we remember fondly a time when things were simpler, less complicated and it appeals to us. Take for example, the way we used to communicate. For some, it was a crank turn for the phone box on the wall and still others recall the old rotary dialed phone with a possible party line where you shared the phone service with a neighbor who might be using the phone at the time you need to. Now it is so different. After a recent FaceTime session with my son and his children, I was reminded that my granddaughter would never know a phone that she cannot see the person she is talking to!

All of these changes and so many others can make the future feel very scary and uncertain so we may feel the need to go back. The Children of Israel seemed to be burdened with this habit and often in times of fear would wish they were back in the slave pits of Egypt—even as horrible as they were. Why? Fear. It is fear that our future cannot be

---

24 Isaiah 54:17 NLT

better than our past. We are not confident that we can adjust to the changes the future will demand from us and so we are tempted to run back to what we know—even if it was once a place of our pain. Remember this. . . .

There's No Going Back Only Forward!

In recent days, I have come to know an amazing woman who is part of our ministry here. She tells a story of brokenness and the ugly scars that marked her former life. Yet, remarkably God has redeemed her brokenness and given her a new future. Her smile tells me that all things are new and that the former things of the past can no longer hurt us, unless we allow them. What God has done, no enemy can stop and in Christ we are free to walk in the newness of God's design for our lives. Sure there will always be moments when the enemy will remind my new friend of all the painful moments and try to intimidate her into believing that she can never be free. Yet in so many ways, she is free and just today she told me, "Bishop, I just erected a monument where all those memories are and I use them to remind me how far God has brought me!" Good for her.

In my first book, *Embracing Destiny*, I talk about the son born to Joseph whose name was Manasseh, which means, *"the Lord has made me forget all my trouble in my Father's house."* It might seem remarkable that one could in fact forget so much hurt and so much pain but with God, all things are possible. I pause to notice a scar on my right hand that reminds of a painful childhood injury that I thought would never heal—but in time it did. Now, many years later, the scar reminds me of what was—but the pain is no longer there. Like my friend, the scars are only monuments, which remind us how far we have come on our journey and how important it is that we not linger in these painful places but keep moving forward to all the plans that God has saved and redeemed us for!

It is for this reason that God beckons us to *Keep Going!*

STAND STILL

Do not deviate from them, turning either to the right or to the left. Then you will be successful in everything you do.[25]

25 Joshua 1:8 NLT

We are all headed somewhere. Where you are right now, is not where you are going—but is simply where you are! We have a tendency to look at life and accept that our present circumstances represent the final chapters of our lives. It is not true! We have a future that is ordained by God and He is bringing us to the fulfillment of that purpose. In time, we will get there—but we must keep going! If we stop . . . if we fail to move ahead with our lives, we will get stuck and we will not see the reality of all that God has planned.

The Children of Israel left Egypt in the middle of the night, excited about the promise of God to bring them to a land that would be their own and would fulfill God's purposes for them. The trip lasted longer than they thought, involved things they were unprepared to handle and caused some of them to give up their hope. In fact, a whole generation of them died in the wilderness because they were unable to keep going despite God's promises.

Life can create some very unusual and uncomfortable realities. Learning to deal with them is part of the journey and in some cases the key to Keep Going!

Some Things You Have To Accept

There is no way to soften the blow that sometimes life gives you results that are not comfortable or even easy to accept. Some of the finest people you know are dealing with stuff that is beyond expectations. A precious couple has been friends for many years and their daughter suffers from a debilitating childhood abnormality that will remain for as long as she lives without a miracle from God. The daily effort of her dedicated mother and father always inspires me. The days always have their challenges and there is no escaping.

I sometimes feel guilty for my own complaining. It seems that there are some things in life you simply have to accept and then move ahead. We might wish they were different and we believe every day for the answers to the prayers we pray. Until that comes, we accept this is the life we have.

Today, I sat with a couple coping with the grief of a child who was taken too quickly from her mother's arms and the grief is smothering for this family. How do we go on? Where is the strength to keep going when life is so hard and so painful? I struggled to provide much comfort today but I do know that in God we have this promise that His strength is ours in life's hardest moments. My friends will make it through this painful valley of death because the Lord is with them and it is His promise that sustains us.

By accepting life as it is we are not denying God's power and though some will contend otherwise, I'm not resigning myself to accept outcomes that are not consistent with God's plans for our lives. Rather, I'm offering the hope that no matter how hard, no matter how lonely, no matter how desperate you are or how empty you feel now, your future is completely overshadowed by the hope of our amazing God who never leaves or forsakes us—ever! In Him, we find the strength to carry on and live each day with hope for our future.

Sometimes Life Can Be Clouded With Fears

Fears are part of life. There is no escaping the fears of life. Though we may try to avoid them and may even deny their existence, dealing with fear is one of the unavoidable challenges of those who choose to live the faith life and move ahead into their God-ordained future. I'm struck that within the one discourse in Joshua 1, there are four mentions of courage in the face of fear for the newly appointed leader. Here is one of the more powerful encouragements.

> Be strong and courageous, for you are the one who will lead these people to possess all the land I swore to their ancestors I would give them. Be strong and very courageous. [26]

God spoke to Joshua about his fears because He knew that fear would be an obstacle. We sometimes act like God doesn't know what is going on around us. It is not uncommon for me to recognize that I have spent my time in prayer catching God up on the details of my life, as if He did not even know! How silly because He knows before I do and when it is necessary, He's already making provisions for the things I have yet to pray to Him about. So when I'm afraid, I must ask myself, what am I afraid? Is it the lack of control I have over the situations and circumstances of my life or is that I don't believe God can take care of me? On the one hand, I am never truly in control of anything in my life—so worry and fear there cannot assist me anyway. One of the funniest verses in the Bible is this one—it always seems to help me smile and balance my worry against God's amazing grace to me.

> Has anyone by fussing in front of the mirror
> ever gotten taller by so much as an inch?[27]

Don't let me mislead you. God knows Joshua will battle fear and He knows that everyone reading this book will at times deal with things that cause them to fear.

No matter what anyone tells you, everybody has things they are afraid of and some of them are strange fears. For me that is my fear of dogs! My friends often tease me but my experience with dogs down through the years has not

---

26 Joshua 1:6-7 NLT
27 Matthew 6:27 Message

helped to alleviate my caution when the canines are present. I've been bitten many times, had stiches from some injuries and generally have come to accept that dogs don't like me. Now you may sleep with your dogs and I'm good with that but respect the fact that it is a real fear to me. May seem strange or aberrant to you, yet each of us has something that strikes fear in our heart. God knows that even if my friends make fun of me!

The reality of life requires that we be proactive in the fight for our faith. So, let's learn to match our fears against the greatness of our God! Here's what I mean. When the people of the Old Testament prayed, it often began something like this. . . .

> Jehoshaphat stood before the community of Judah and Jerusalem in front of the new courtyard at the Temple of the Lord. He prayed, "O Lord, God of our ancestors, you alone are the God who is in heaven. You are ruler of all the kingdoms of the earth. You are powerful and mighty; no one can stand against you! O our God, did you not drive out those who lived in this land when your people Israel arrived? And did you not give this land forever to the descendants of your friend Abraham? Your people settled here and built this Temple to honor your name. They said, 'Whenever we are faced with any calamity such as war, plague, or famine, we can come to stand in your presence before this Temple where your name is honored. We can cry out to you to save us, and you will hear us and rescue us.'[28]

It was a rehearsal of the greatness of God, plain and simple. Here the king is about to ask God to intervene against a band of invaders who threaten the kingdom and against whom he knows he does not have enough weapons or warriors. His desperation is apparent and yet he reminds himself, those who hear him and in essence the God to whom he prays that His best ally is the testimony of a faithful God!

---

28 2 Chronicles 20:5-9 NLT

Jehoshaphat prays like a man who has known the power of God to deliver before.

We should do that. We should lay our fears out before the Lord and test them against the awesomeness of our God—who has provided for us each and every day and whose grace enables our lives. When we do, we will find our fears are less ominous and in fact, completely impotent in view of this powerful God. Who compares to the greatness of our God? Who could rival His power and goodness? Of course, we know or should that God is bigger than our fears and more than enough to take care of ANYTHING we could face!

Sometimes Life Demands Bold Faith

Here is what Joshua heard from the Lord, *"This is my command—be strong and courageous! Do not be afraid or discouraged. For the Lord your God is with you wherever you go."*[29] He had no way of knowing just what that would mean or how that would mark the steps of his new journey God was calling him to. All he had was the promise of Divine Presence and the memory of a God who did amazing things before his very eyes.

There are moments when your faith just has to be stand up and be counted. One such moment for me came in 2005 while I lived in Baton Rouge, Louisiana and was leading the state ministries of the Church of God there. We had been involved for a couple of years with missionary work in the country of Honduras and had made numerous trips to help with work at orphanages, building schools, planting churches and supporting other benevolent ministries. Our annual summer convention was approaching and I decided

29 Joshua 1:9 NLT

we would make a bold statement for our missions' effort and raise an offering of cash for the churches of Honduras. In my planning sessions with my leaders, I laid out the plan for a missions offering of ten thousand dollars cash on that one night, asking churches and pastors to bring their offering to the meeting for a show of support. When I mentioned the amount, one man whistled and said "that will be some offering!" and as soon as he did, I felt God quicken me with this question, "IS THAT ALL YOU ARE GOING TO ASK ME FOR? YOU COULD DO THAT MUCH WITHOUT ME." It was like a Gideon moment when God reminded him that with 32,000 the report would not be what God had done but what Gideon had done. I immediately felt ashamed that I had not trusted God more and blurted out, "let's go for $50,000 instead!" My team was stunned and yet there was something at work in them and me that demanded the moment. They felt it and I did as well. So the plan was to raise the offering goal to $50,000. In the months leading up, the enemy began to tempt me with accusations that were designed to steal my faith. The condemnation came to my mind that I was leading the people to failure and such disappointment would break their spirits when the offering did not match the goal. I kept praying and working, holding to the prompting that God was demanding bold faith that would seize the moment.

The night of the offering came and I stood in front of the people with mixed emotions—so excited about what could be and yet wondering what I would say if it did not happen. The people began to bring the offerings to the front and I waited as the finance committee counted the offerings. When they brought me the total, I jumped to my feet interrupting the speaker to announce the total—$53,000 in cash!

A celebration erupted in the church and we rejoiced over what had been accomplished. It was a defining moment but we just did not even know.

Three months later, Hurricane Katrina would blow through Louisiana with winds in excess of 150 miles per hour and thirty of our churches would be closed temporarily or destroyed completely. We were devastated but like King Jehoshaphat we began to remind ourselves of this God who has always been so faithful. During the next two years, God sent more than one million dollars through our offices and churches to repair all but one of the churches and rebuild the people into a mighty army for the Kingdom. I will always believe the seeds of that recovery, though we did not know it, were birthed in that planning meeting when we responded to God's demand for bold faith in impossible opportunities. God may, in fact be calling you to greatness through a demand for bold and unshakeable faith.

God's promise for the land was secure but the people would be forced to engage themselves and demonstrate a bold faith in order to gain the reality of the promise. Crossing the Jordan River and conquering the walled city of Jericho would take more than religious platitudes—it would take a bold faith that embraced the opportunities set before them, despite what it appeared to be. Only as God's power was demonstrated through the people and before them would Jericho's walls fall. There is not enough firepower in Joshua's arsenal to get it done. Neither is there in yours or mine. Each and every day, we are completely dependent on the Lord for the energy, grace and power to move forward with our lives.

Remember this, the easy thing in life is to give up and the world is filled with those who have chosen to quit pursuing their promise . . . but the future is before us and we only get there if we *Keep Going!*

WALKING BLINDLY

*No one will be able to stand against
you as long as you live. For I will be
with you as I was with Moses. I will
not fail you or abandon you.*[30]

---
30 Joshua 1:5 NLT

Y ou rise in the night to go to the bathroom and in your semi-sleep state, you stumble into the furniture or the door casing, stubbing a toe or bruising your knee. The problem was not your inability to walk; it was the fact that in the darkened room, your bearings were not as clear as they would be in the daylight. Ever walk into a dark room and even if it is a room with which you are familiar, you still are stopped by the sheer darkness of the room? You know how the drill works. You have to stand still long enough that your eyes begin adjust to the amount of light available to you. What you find is that there is more visibility in the room than you might think—you simply have to adjust to it.

Fears that keep us from moving forward

Fear is a paralyzing feeling when it grips you. Some of you reading this book know all too well what I'm writing about. Fear can have a crippling effect on life and it's normal patterns. I've documented in other works, how I have chosen to engage the battle against my own fears and their impact on me. The Scriptures tell us that fear is torment and when fear is fully at work in us, it is because we don't believe in God's love for us, as we should! As we embrace God's love, we are not afraid. There is no fear in love and the power of God's love moves fear to the backburner of our hearts. That's what the Bible says. I try to live by that every day—I'm sure you do as well. Yet, more times than I'm proud to admit, fears run upon me and give me pause.

We cannot simply ignore the fact that Joshua is told four times to be courageous and not to fear. Why? I think it's because God knows the human heart's tendency is to fear. When things are tough and overpowering, fear will creep in and we are tempted to allow our fears to run unchecked.

When that happens, it sometimes creates unhealthy responses physically and even spiritually. For those who are choosing the path to keep going in life and to move beyond these moments here, fear will be an enemy. It was for Joshua and the people he would lead and it was for his fathers who preceded him. In fact, the group he is leading are descended from those whose fear caused them NOT to inherit the land.

The story is found in Numbers 13 and involves the generations, which came out of Egypt and have been traveling through the wilderness on the way to the Promised Land. Once they reach the region of Kadish Barnea, God instructs Moses to send twelve spies into the land and to bring back a report to the people of the land they are going to inhabit. The spies return with evidence of the fruitfulness of the land and what they saw. Ten of the spies share a negative and frightful report of the giants and their assessment that the people of God will never live there because of what they saw. Two spies, Joshua and Caleb, encourage the people to put their trust in the Lord and know that God will bring them to the land. However, the people believed the negative report and began lamenting and complaining that they would have been better off to remain in Egypt as slaves! This angers God so much that He announces that the entire generation will die in the wilderness and that it will be their children who will inherit the land. This was Joshua and the generation that he is leading into the land.

Why was God so angry? Did He not anticipate the fear of the people? Yes, God knows our weak frame and how easily we tend to rush to fear. I think what angered God so much is how forgetful the people were as to how God had faithfully taken care of them in every situation they had faced. It was God's hand that defeated their enemies. It was God's faithfulness and provision that provided for the food, clothing and protection. All they had was what God had given them. Now, in this moment, they act like God cannot take care of them anymore.

Just like me.

There are moments that dot my life and point to occasions when I forget the faithfulness of God expressed in my life. I fail to remember that God has provided for me EVERY time and that nothing I am or have, came by the extension of my power or might. It is God who has kept me and enabled my life. How could I forget that? Sadly I do and in failing to remember, I become afraid. It is the fear that my health will fail without warning and I won't be able to afford health-care. It is the fear that life will become too expensive for me to live comfortably. It is the fear that I cannot protect my children from the things in life that may cause them pain. It is the fear that I will be alone. The list continues. . . .

So God says to Joshua—**This is my command—be strong and courageous! Do not be afraid or discouraged. For the Lord your God is with you wherever you go.**[31] It is a straightforward word to the new leader with a BIG assignment and it is a fresh reminder to you and me. The Lord is with us in every moment, every situation and every circumstance that may cause us to fear. Fear cripples our progress. We cannot keep going into the future God has or-dained if fear is holding us back—and it always does.

Fear of failure

My colleague, Larry never fully appreciated how gifted he was or the potential of his life because he was so afraid

---

that he would disappoint others and me. He played it safe always and never allowed himself to risk—ever! He often told me that some people live for the limelight and others stay on the sidelines but all are on the team. Well, God cannot completely use a life paralyzed by the fear that our efforts will not be enough or that we might fail. Such fear assumes that the kingdom is dependent on my ability or accomplishments but in reality this is not about what I can do but how God works through me. Nothing that I can do will be enough. Only as I present myself to him am I able to be what He chooses!

All of us fail regularly. I'm not speaking of spiritual things only but failure is a common part of our lives. In baseball, a Hall of Fame player fails as much as 70% of the time at the plate. It is important to note that most innovative discoveries are the result of many failed attempts. Failure after failure kept Alexander Graham Bell working to find the right combination to make the telephone work. Had he allowed the fear that he might fail to dominate, he would have limited his potential to move ahead to the next BIG moment in his life and as such, that moment defined life for you and me even today!

Yet, I do fear that my efforts are not enough and try as I might, my heart can sometimes be overwhelmed to the point that I struggle with whether my inadequacies are disappointing Him. It's a performance based spiritual anxiety that is not rooted in the true love of God because His love is not predicated on what I do but who I am. For Him, my worship is about who He is and not what He does. Why is that so hard for us to grasp? Joshua has an overwhelming assignment but an amazing God has called him whose strength and power surpasses all obstacles. As Joshua will find, there is no task that is bigger than the God who calls him. In like manner, we can always know that our moments of fear are swallowed up in the victory that comes from the knowledge of God's incredible power. Remember what God said?

> No one will be able to stand against you as long as you live. For I will be with you as I was with Moses. I will not fail you or abandon you.[32]

Insecurity is a powerful force in the human mind. As we try to assess our own abilities and potential, it is easy to be overcome by the fears that we are not enough for the task. Moses was such a man, so insecure in his own abilities that he bargained with God for someone else to be given the assignment to go to Pharaoh and ask for the release of God's people. What Moses did not appreciate nor do we at times, is that God is not looking for our ability but our availability and our willingness to let Him do what only He can do, through us.

What God accomplished in Moses was amazing because at some point, Moses surrendered to the notion that God at work in Him was immeasurably more capable than he was alone. It is the principle that Paul writes about to the Ephesian believers,

> Now all glory to God, who is able, through his mighty power at work within us, to accomplish infinitely more than we might ask or think.[33]

Fears of the future

The headlines of each day offer ominous thoughts and fear about what will be tomorrow and how we might cope with our new world. With news cycles that are around the

---

32 Joshua 1:5 NLT
33 Ephesians 3:20 NLT

clock and global in scope, we find that we are increasingly bombarded by news of what is happening thousands of miles away in contexts that are foreign and foreboding. Sometimes that separation only further heightens our fears about what is coming to the earth. I'm beginning to wonder if it is even necessary for me to know so much about things that are so far away from me. The uncertainty of life is always a part of our life journey and while we may wish that we could establish security in this life, we can't. Life is unpredictable on so many levels. We can never find our hope or the strength to live in this uncertain world by looking to this life for our security.

Life can change without warning! Shelley Yutzy knows that all too well. Her pastor husband left a local nursing home one Sunday afternoon, where he had just ministered and he phoned his wife that he would soon be home. She prepared his dinner and waited for him to arrive. When he did not come in a reasonable time, she worried something was not right. Her instincts were on target. That day, Pastor Lutrell Yutzy was killed in a single vehicle accident when he lost control of his truck and it rolled over on him as it left the road. From a courtesy phone call from her husband to planning his funeral in minutes, Shelley is left to manage her life now alone. Life is so very unpredictable.

So where is the hope? How can we live without unreasonable fears amidst so much uncertainty? It is this simple truth—OUR HOPE IS IN THE CERTAINTY OF OUR GOD! He is the dependable One and in all of life's most difficult moments, it is the faithfulness of our God that sustains us. No other anchor can hold us. No other resource will be sufficient. No matter what you face or what you encounter in this life, God is enough. His forever presence will keep you going!

There is no way that Joshua can stand in the presence of God, hearing the assignment and not have some thoughts about what will happen, what will be coming and how will he face it. Yet, God knows that about him and consistently reminds him of Divine Presence and encourages him to build faith and confidence in the Lord. So must we. Our eyes on the future must be coupled with our hearts surrendered to the God who sees and manages it all. The reports of global conflict are not news to God. He knew it before it happened and since He sees it all in the context from beginning to the end, He knows that all is well. He refreshes our spirits when we cease our fretting over things we cannot control or influence anyway an simply rest in the peace that comes from knowing God is always near and always on top of the situation.

Joshua cannot know at the time how God is setting up the journey to possess the land. He does not know that in Jericho is a woman whose faith in God is building and whose conviction is to be on the Lord's side. God is preparing her to play a role in the future God is ordaining for Joshua and the people. He does not yet know how God is already planning to bring down those intimidating walls of Jericho and allow His people to achieve a mighty conquest. So, he must believe in what he cannot see and trust in what he cannot know. What he can know and build his confidence in is the promise that was given to him and in times of fear and anxiety, when life is not as we desire, we can know that we are not alone, not ever!

On the night before the biggest leadership moment of his life, Joshua had an unexpected visitor. It was a simple

reminder of what God has already promised. God is like
that. He will provide a word of instruction or help and then
come back around to reinforce and encourage us. He did for
Joshua here.

> When Joshua was near the town of Jericho, he looked up and saw
> a man standing in front of him with sword in hand. Joshua went
> up to him and demanded, "Are you friend or foe?" "Neither one,"
> he replied. "I am the commander of the Lord's army."
>
> At this, Joshua fell with his face to the ground in reverence. "I am
> at your command," Joshua said. "What do you want your servant
> to do?" The commander of the Lord's army replied, "Take off
> your sandals, for the place where you are standing is holy." And
> Joshua did as he was told.[34]

The dialogue was exactly what Joshua needed.

He was not alone. Neither are we.

Keep Going!

34 Joshua 5:13-15 NLT

LEANING FORWARD

*" . . . the time has come for you to lead these people, the Israelites, **across the Jordan River into the land** I am giving them. I promise you what I promised Moses: 'wherever you set foot, you will be on land I have given you"*[35]

---

35 Joshua 1:3-4 NLT (emphasis mine)

There is a forward press in my spirit. I sense God is calling me. I'm not alone. Others are sensing a fresh drawing to new places of relationship and commitment to God's plans and purposes. What I mean by this is that we are leaning into the promises of God, straining to grasp all that God has planned. We are eager to learn and understand His purposes for our lives. We find our meaning in the plans God has made for our lives because we know the character of God and by experience have learned we can trust Him!

Zacchaeus was a man with a troubled past. He had become very wealthy because he collected taxes and in the eyes of his fellow countrymen had done so through questionable means. Yet, when word comes to him that the famous and mysterious teacher from Galilee was to pass near where he was, Zacchaeus made a determined effort to see him. He was short of stature, so his efforts were more extreme than usual. He found a tree and climbed up to get a good look. From where he was perched, he felt sure he would be able to get a clear view of this man others were talking about. There was excitement as he anticipated the experience he had planned for himself.

He simply had no idea what he was in store for! When Jesus passed by the tree, He stopped and amazingly called Zacchaeus by name. Not only that, he invited himself to Zacchaeus' home. Can you imagine the excitement with which he and Jesus moved to the house? This was not what Zacchaeus had anticipated, in fact, it was far more than he could have ever dreamed of. Needless to say, it caused no little stir in the town as local citizens angrily complained— *"He has gone to be the guest of a notorious sinner," they grumbled* and they were right! Zacchaeus was a sinner and well known at that.

Here's my point. Life is before us and we can choose to live again and move beyond our pain, sorrow or obstacles or we can accept the attitude that life cannot improve or be as it should be. The choice is ours. If we choose to lean forward and find joy again, the opportunities will be greater than we imagine. In such cases, it seems God rewards those who make the effort to find Him. Think of the stories of Scripture where individuals were so eager to find Him that they took extraordinary measures to see and meet Jesus.

I think of Blind Bartimaeus who determined he would meet Jesus and despite those who sought to quell his enthusiasm, he cried with a loud voice until Jesus stopped and answered both his call and his request. A former blind man was changed because he chose to lean forward to find Jesus. How differently would his life had been had he not pressed ahead, despite all to encounter the Christ?

I think of a woman whose past twelve years were filled with a hemorrhage that would not stop and while doctors and friends gave her no hope, she heard of Jesus and determined that at all costs, she would try and touch Him. She risked much but she did touch His garments and the transformation was immediate and she was healed. Jesus told her that it was her faith that brought her relief. She simply refused to be denied and that forward lean of her heart changed the rest of her life. Would her life not have been filled with deep regret had she allowed outside influences to dissuade her from the press in her spirit to do the unthinkable—touch Jesus and allow her unshakeable faith to be the catalyst for life change?

I think of Nicodemus, a Jewish ruler whose interest in Jesus was such that at great risk he came seeking, under cover of night, to learn more. What he found was a discourse with the Savior of the world and the personal invitation to new birth. Nicodemus was forever changed. When I read this passage, my heart is strangely stirred to realize how much his forward lean to find Jesus transformed him.

> Afterward Joseph of Arimathea, who had been a secret disciple of Jesus (because he feared the Jewish leaders), asked Pilate for permission to take down Jesus' body. When Pilate gave permission, Joseph came and took the body away. With him came Nicodemus, the man who had come to Jesus at night. He brought about seventy-five pounds of perfumed ointment made from myrrh and aloes. Following Jewish burial custom, they wrapped Jesus' body with the spices in long sheets of linen cloth.[36]

Don't try to tell me that the man was not changed! Like Nicodemus, in our hearts, there is an insatiable hunger to regain, restore and rekindle our spirits by leaning forward to the life God has purposed for us. We may have experienced loss. We may have suffered much in our physical bodies. Life may have been terribly hard. We may be marked by bitter experiences but the desire to know Him, to find Him is never taken away.

Think for a moment and ponder how differently your life would have been had you been willing to risk more—to venture more faith—to take more chances with God. There is an adage that says at the end of our lives we will not regret the chances we took but the moments we were afraid to risk. I don't want to live that way. In fact, I choose not to live that way! Faith is about risk. Faith in God and His plans for our lives is ultimate risk!

The alternative is to simply allow ourselves to be drowned in the mire of unmet expectations, hurts and disappointments of our past experiences and sorrow that never ends. While we are tempted at times to think that our lives are

36 John 19:38-40 NLT

some sort of punitive action of an angry God or that God has chosen not to work in our behalf, our hearts know that this is not true! Life is hard and while none of us have explanations for why some suffer more than others and sorrow seems more prevalent in your house than in your neighbors, we know that in all things God is just and present to help us with all that life brings.

A young woman named Lisa just lost her son to a seizure that took him almost instantly. It's not the first child Lisa has given up. In fact, her father tells me that Lisa has lost several children through miscarriages and other physical challenges. The fact this son lived twenty years is both a medical miracle and a strong and painful reminder of how much loss has marked Lisa's life. She wants to believe and yet her pain tells her God is not working for her but against her. Why would God allow so much heartache? Like you, I wish I could replace her pain with joy. I wish my words were magical and cancelled the hurt she is experiencing. I have nothing but the companionship of prayer and my faith that though life is hard, God is good and always near. I'm praying Lisa finds that and does not lose her faith as she continues to press ahead with her life journey.

When I am still and allow my heart to listen closely, I sense God saying to me that the journey is ahead and there is nothing to linger for in the pain of our past. It may feel to you that the destination of joy that you seek is so far away as to be unreachable—it's not! In fact, you are closer to your desires than you might think. Listen to your heart. John Eldridge's book *Desire*[37] has been a particular favorite of mine this year. After reading it and allowing John to speak to my own heart about the attitudes there, I began a search with

God to understand my heart—what is contained there—why my motivation is what it is. It was a painful, exhausting but exciting experience.

Among the things I found is a profound desire to have what God wants me to have. That requires me to know Him more intimately and to be willing to encounter the moments when He makes me challenge what is truly in my heart. At times, I'm ashamed of what He allows me to see about myself but at the same time, His amazing love is not condemning my heart but restoring it. When I come to want what God wants for me, then the pressures of my own pursuits are emptied and melted into the things that make me genuinely happy—and that is the greatest discovery of my experience after reading *Desire*.

We Cannot Create Our Own Happiness.

I guess it would be simpler, if we could generate our own happiness, but we can't and the more we attempt to do so, the more frustrated we are. Take King Solomon as an example, he became exhausted trying to be happy—to find something that would satisfy the insatiable appetite for happiness that is in all of us. Some seek to find happiness in destructive habits that only cripple the body or inflict unnecessary pain. Still others believe the pursuit of happiness comes in the experience of pleasure but in time they find that the emptiness of their pleasure-seeking requires more and more and they are never fully satisfied.

Jesus encountered Satan in the wilderness and from the narrative come several important reminders that frame this thought for us. In the one temptation, Satan appeals to the human hunger that nags at Jesus and he invites Jesus to use his power to create something that satisfies. Jesus saw it for

what it was—a substitute for the kind of life God wants
us all to have. He most certainly could have turned those
loaves into bread. Jesus had the power and the authority to
do that. Yet, he rightly discerned that loaves of bread are not
the path to happiness and He responds,

> Man shall not live on bread alone, but on every
> word that proceeds out of the mouth of God.[38]

I wish happiness were that simple. Just calling it down
like Elijah's fire. Rather, we know that true happiness is a
relationship with Christ, a giving of ourselves and all we are
to Him and the complete surrender enables us to find our
joy in Him.

In another temptation, Satan invites Jesus to tempt God—
to make God prove Himself. Jesus refused and demonstrates
for us that God is not on trial in our lives as we navigate.
Our lives have never been about whether God can or will do
what we want but how we position our own desires to be in
alignment with His. The longer we serve Him, the less we
come to need Him to perform for us. At first, we seek a God
who gives us answers to a test we did not study for or helps
us get a date with the boy who ignores us. Later, we promise
to serve Him, if he helps us get the promotion, or the raise
or protects our children from the vices of drugs. However,
in time we realize our relationship with Him is never about
Him proving His powers but about our hearts finding true
happiness in alignment. We come to surrender and maybe
that is the ultimate scope of our life's journey—the total and
complete surrender of our hearts to Him, His will and His
plans. His own Son knelt in the Garden that fateful night

---

38 Matthew 4:4 NASB

and provided an amazing example of the path to true happiness when he prayed,

> "My Father! If it is possible, let this cup of suffering be taken away from me. Yet I want your will to be done, not mine."[39]

We may never understand the ways of God but we can know that God is bigger than our own moments and His amazing faithfulness is the testimony of our life.

The Hope We Seek Is Closer Than We Know

Jeremiah was a weeping prophet and his writings provide a snapshot of a man deeply troubled and bewildered by the way God has treated him. At times, he despised the call of God upon his life and he has wept over the demise of his land and the suffering of God's people. So when I read his penned words here, I get the sense of how deeply he draws from the wells of God's provision for those who need hope in dark hours. He writes,

> I'll never forget the trouble, the utter lostness, the taste of ashes, the poison I've swallowed. I remember it all—oh, how well I remember—the feeling of hitting the bottom. But there's one other thing I remember, and remembering, I keep a grip on hope: God's loyal love couldn't have run out, his merciful love couldn't have dried up. They're created new every morning. How great your faithfulness! I'm sticking with God (I say it over and over). He's all I've got left.[40]

Maybe that's the way you feel at this moment. The troubles, the loneliness, the emptiness of your life is smothering and you cannot seem to find your way out of the dark hole you attempting to climb out of. Take heart—hope is nearer than you could know.

---

39   Matthew 26:39 NLT
40   Lamentations 3:19-24 The Message

One day in my room as I prepared to dress for work, this song began to play and in its words came a powerful message from the Lord to me—you just have to keep going—even when you don't feel like it or even know where you are supposed to go. Despite the emotions that betray us and the questions for which no answers seem readily available, we must go on. As we close this chapter, read the words slowly and may God grant you the understanding that He is right where He has always been. . . .

> There always seems to be a door that you can't open
> There always seems to be a mountain you can't climb
> But you keep on reaching—You just keep on reaching
> When your destiny is out there in the distance
> But the road ahead's a minefield in disguise
> And you keep on moving—You just keep on moving
> You will make it through this
> Just give it time
> You gotta give it time
> This is what you're made for
> Standing in the downpour
> Knowing that the sun will shine
> Forget what lies behind you
> Heaven walks beside you
> You got to give it one more try
> One more time
> You just keep on reaching
> You just keep on, you keep on moving
> When the shadows fall on everything you're dreaming
> When the promises turn out to be a lie
> You just keep believing—You just keep believing
> Oh, don't stop your dreaming
> It's gonna be alright—It's gonna be alright
> You've got to keep on reaching
> Keep believing
> It's gonna be alright [41]

---

41 http://www.metrolyrics.com/one-more-time-lyrics-michael-w-smith.html

Your God is the hope you are searching for. In Him, you find the strength to keep going and to move forward with your life, in complete faith that God's plans transcend the now moments of your life. His purposes are bigger, greater and more in control of your future than you could know. He is directing the steps you are taking—don't be afraid any longer. He's got you . . . so . . . ***Keep Going!***

DESTINATION

"This is my command—be strong and courageous! Do not be afraid or discouraged. For the Lord your God is with you wherever you go."[42]

---

42 Joshua 1:9 NLT

The end of a journey is bittersweet. There is the euphoria of arrival and the reality that one's travel has ended. However, that can sometimes be the bitter part because the journey itself is the larger piece of the destination—getting there—enduring and persevering to the end. I think, in part, that is due to the effort the journey entails and the motivation that reaching the destination brings. It seems to be that way with the people Joshua has been leading through the conquest of the land.

Forty years is a long time and when they left Egypt that fateful night when every first born in the land, of human and animal died, they had no idea how long the journey would take. They were excited and armed with the anticipation of their new home and a future they could only imagine. Now the years have taken their toll and the journey has been filled with many ups and downs. Some have not made it, having passed along the way, some by the judgment of God. However, they have not given up and have simply kept moving by the will and plan of God and now they find themselves on the brink of realizing their greatest anticipation.

I look back fondly on some incredible seasons of my life. I still recall with clarity the difficulty of the journey and how hard I worked to get to the conclusion of the assignment. Yet, I also remember how fulfilled I was to reach my goals. I once worked for a man who was sick but few people knew it at the time. A close group of us worked in the office with him and made a commitment both as a group and individually to use our strongest efforts to help him reach the finish line of his career. Looking back, those were some of the hardest and yet now, some of the most rewarding days of my life. The goal was clear—our friend was weak and needed us. No effort was too much. During those years, we constantly reminded each other that our objectives were noble and worthy and we put our heads down and worked toward our goal. When it was over, there was the most amazing sense of accomplishment and while few people even knew the depth of personal sacrifice many on our team made, we were satisfied that it was all good.

In the summer of 1976, I stood in the parking lot of a Dallas, Texas restaurant and informed my mother that I would not be returning to college that fall. I knew she would take it hard because one of the reasons she had gone back to work was to help pay for my college education. I was young and knew better than others what was best and going back to school was not high on my list of things to do. However, I did make her a promise at the time that I would finish and graduate. She seemed accepting of my promise but looking back now, I had no idea what that commitment would cost me in time, energy and effort. The years came and went and I became deeply engaged in many other pursuits and gave little thought to the promise I made to her that day. One day in 1994, I opened an envelope of a young student who sent me a graduation announcement and while I had gotten many such announcements in the mail, this one caught my attention and the question was—when will your mother get the announcement of the fulfillment of your promise? It struck me that there was unfinished work ahead and so with the assistance of good advisors, I got on track with online learning environments and thirteen years later, I stood as the "old man" in the group of young twenty-somethings walking across the stage to shake the college president's hand and receive my diploma. My mother was there that day and there was joy in knowing I had finished what I promised.

Life is difficult. I know that and so do you. No one knows the future they will face as they live. You take each day as it comes. You handle the challenges and move on. It is a quest to reach the destination we have been made for. This earthly existence is not our destiny. We have been made eternal and while we cannot fully appreciate what that means, we just know that we must get there no matter what it takes. There is a scene in the movie *The Mission* where a missionary is seen carrying an enormous load to the top of the mountain where the village lies and the struggle is difficult. The on-lookers know little about the man except the courage and determination he demonstrates to reach his destination. The strong message I drew in viewing was that often the destination is more important than the struggle. I'm always moved by the visional imagery of his struggle to reach the village, despite the load and the obstacles he faced You get the sense he has counted the cost as much as he could and determined that the struggle must be engaged and is worth his strongest efforts. The missionary knows that. So do we.

There must be more to this life than what we now see. In our hearts, we sense this deeply and we know that this is not all there is to our existence and future. The Apostle Paul once said, " . . . *if our hope in Christ is only for this life, we are more to be pitied than anyone in the world.*"[43] There is a crush of daily life that moves our hearts to believe for another day, another place. We are confident we will reach it. We shall make it to heaven. All in due time.

Sometimes I wonder what heaven must be like. There is no sickness there. There is no death. There is no sin. I like to say heaven is life as God intended it to be before sin entered the world. If so, then heaven will be fun, fulfilling and it will

_____
43 1 Corinthians 15:19 NLT

be worth our every effort. So much of what wears us down and exhausts our hearts will not be part of heaven. So many of our loved ones are already there. I cannot wait!

Just today, a mother who lost her baby in the middle of her pregnancy grapples with her grief and writes to me of her questions about what is the fate of her baby in heaven. She wonders if her baby knows others there and what if anything those persons already there know about what we are going through here. I don't have answers for her, though she may think so. What I do know and strongly believe is that heaven is going to be worth it and those of our loved ones already there will be waiting on our arrival.

I was blessed to have four amazing grandparents. My mom's parents were salt of the earth people. My grandfather *Grampy* was such an honorable man and while his faith in God came later in life, he was a shiny example of what I want to be. *Grammy* was the glue of her family, an industrious and hard working woman who willed herself to greatness in my eyes. Never wavering, in good times and bad, she set her face to live on this earth in ways that honored God and her family. When she passed, I was invited to provide a family eulogy among the few remaining friends that were there. She had lived so long that most of her contemporaries were already passed. I remember thinking about how Grammy had made it to heaven and how much heaven would have meant to her. She was adopted at an early age and struggled to understand why her birthparents had given her away. She had very little in her early life and while she worked hard and helped provide a home and necessities for her husband and three children, life was often hard. Yet, she persevered and she made it. Heaven was surely more than she could have possibly imagined.

Like my Grammy, each of us is moving toward a destination that is beyond this moment. This place where we are now is not heaven . . . not by any stretch of the imagination! I don't care how good your life may be now; this is not the place to which your journey ends. God has prepared for you another place and by God's grace you will get there. It may not feel like it now and the road is hard and difficult but you have to keep going with faith and confidence in the future ahead.

Have you ever watched a person pass from this life? The human body fights against the passing because we were made to be eternal and death is an enemy to the creation. Yet, there comes a point at which the body resigns to the larger call of eternity and the spirit is given up to God. Sometimes you will hear people say, *"I'm tired and I'm just ready to go home!"* The hope of our hearts is to survive this life and make it to the other side, regardless. There must be a steely determination that nothing can be allowed to steal the hope of our hearts. We are going there.

Joshua is given a simple command. Lead the people to possess the land God promised them. Sounds simple, right? It's not. The journey will have many twists and turns and at times the load will be heavy and even the strongest will be tempted to turn back but the encouragement of the Lord is strong. . . .

After the death of Moses the servant of God, God spoke to Joshua, Moses' assistant:

> "Moses my servant is dead. Get going. Cross this Jordan River, you and all the people. Cross to the country I'm giving to the People of Israel. I'm giving you every square inch of the land you set your foot on—just as I promised Moses. From the wilderness and this Lebanon east to the Great River, the Euphrates

River—all the Hittite country—and then west to the Great Sea. *It's all yours.*[44]

I'm absolutely confident I cannot do justice to the promise of heaven that God has given to you and me. What I can say is that those persons whom God has allowed to have insight regarding it have amazing and wonderful things to say. Here are few I love to read. . . .

> "No eye has seen, no ear has heard, and no mind has imagined what God has prepared for those who love him."[45]

> "Don't let this throw you. You trust God, don't you? Trust me. There is plenty of room for you in my Father's home. If that weren't so, would I have told you that I'm on my way to get a room ready for you? And if I'm on my way to get your room ready, I'll come back and get you so you can live where I live.[46]

> "Look, I am coming soon, bringing my reward with me to repay all people according to their deeds. I am the Alpha and the Omega, the First and the Last, the Beginning and the End."[47]

> Behold, I stand at the door and knock; if anyone hears My voice and opens the door, I will come in to him and will dine with him, and he with Me. He who overcomes, I will grant to him to sit down with Me on My throne, as I also overcame and sat down with My Father on His throne.[48]

The streets in heaven are gold . . . really! There is a tree in heaven that bears fruit all the year and the leaves are healing to the inhabitants of heaven. The gates are pearl and while I've never seen pearl gates, I have seen pearls on a necklace and they are stunning. Yet, heaven is not about natural beauty and breathtaking views, though all of that will be special. Heaven is about those who reside there. Jesus, our Savior is

---

44   Joshua 1:1-4 NLT Emphasis mine.

45   1 Corinthians 2:9 NLT

46   John 14:1-3 The Message

47   Revelation 22:12-13 NLT

48   Revelation 3:20-21 NASB

there. Our loved ones are there. The saints of the Scriptures
are there along with all those who have lived before us who
trusted in the Lord as we do, choosing not to be kept from
the journey God had set before them. Through every moment, good and bad, they kept going. In doing so, they came
to the end of the journey and made it to the other side. We
will as well . . . if we keep going!

The passage in Joshua 1, that has been our point of refer-
ence, begins with this announcement—*"Now it came about
after the death of Moses the servant of the Lord . . ."* and is
followed next by God's startling words to Joshua—*"Moses
my servant is dead. Therefore, the time has come for you
to lead these people, the Israelites, across the Jordan River into the land I am giving them."*[49] Moses was Joshua's
teacher—the man who had once anointed and laid his hands
of spiritual approval on Joshua's head. Such an announcement must have come as a huge emotional hit.

I've thought some about Moses and those final hours of
his life before he passed away. The narrative and timeline
are fascinating to me. It gets very interesting at the conclusion of a moment of fatherly instruction from Moses to the
People of Israel,

> When Moses had finished reciting all these words to the people
> of Israel, he added: "Take to heart all the words of warning I
> have given you today. Pass them on as a command to your chil-
> dren so they will obey every word of these instructions. These
> instructions are not empty words—they are your life! By obey-
> ing them you will enjoy a long life in the land you will occupy
> when you cross the Jordan River."[50]

When he finished, then God spoke these instructions to
Moses. . . .

49   Joshua 1:1, 3 NLT
50   Deuteronomy 32:45-47 NLT

> ***That same day*** the Lord said to Moses, "Go to Moab, to the
> mountains east of the river, and climb Mount Nebo, which is
> across from Jericho. Look out across the land of Canaan, the land
> I am giving to the people of Israel as their own special posses-
> sion. Then *you will die there on the mountain.* You will join your
> ancestors, just as Aaron, your brother, died on Mount Hor and
> joined his ancestors.[51]

It feels heavy to me that Moses hears these words from
God after all that has taken place in his life but then I'm
thinking like a human. The ending of life on this side of
heaven is all that I've ever witnessed. I don't know what it
is like to reach the other side. I do know the impact of realizing that life is ending here for individuals I have loved,
those I have labored with, people who mattered to me. It's
the reason I sympathize with the impact of the announcement to Joshua.

Walter Atkinson was a spiritual father to me. When his
health failed and the end was near, one of his daughters
called me and put him on the phone. His voice was weak
and there was little strength. It was time for him to go home
and he said as much to me that day. There was sadness and
I wept tears as I listened to his goodbye but there was also
the realization that this was the destination that his journey had been pointed to for many years. When I hung up, I
knew I would not see my mentor again and there were more
tears. Later that week, I stood with many others and began
the accepting process that life here is not what I'm looking
for. It's too painful to separate, too difficult to handle the
sorrow. I spoke at his funeral and in those moments felt the
bittersweet taste of goodbye and the joy I hoped heaven was
for a dear and good friend. I'm not sure what he's doing now

---

51 Deuteronomy 32:48-50 NLT (emphasis mine)

or how much of what is happening with me he may know. If he could know, I would wish him to know how much he is missed and how much I want to be where he is—where my loved ones are—where Jesus is!

Moses and Joshua knew how I felt. When he left the camp and they parted ways, Joshua probably knew the farewell was final on this earth and so as Moses fades into the distant horizon, the resignation of what would be next, how does one go on, surely filled Joshua's mind. With the people he waited to know that Moses was indeed gone. In time, God made the official announcement but God also gave Joshua this instruction—" . . . **the time has come for you to lead these people.**" It is a powerful visual for me. Sad, though he was, Joshua had to keep going. There was no other choice. As much as he loved Moses, the journey for Joshua and those who remained continued. So does mine and while there are seldom days when Walter does not come to mind, I'm still here and there is a purpose and destiny to my life. I've got to keep going and that is what the Lord seemed to whisper in my spirit as I sat in my hotel room in Brazil that early morning. Life continues and by accepting that, the window of opportunity for life is opened again.

> Then Moses went up to Mount Nebo from the plains of Moab and climbed Pisgah Peak, which is across from Jericho. And the Lord showed him the whole land, from Gilead as far as Dan; **all** the land of Naphtali; the land of Ephraim and Manasseh; all the land of Judah, extending to the Mediterranean Sea the Negev; the Jordan Valley with Jericho—the city of palms—as far as Zoar. Then the Lord said to Moses, "This is the land I promised on oath to Abraham, Isaac, and Jacob when I said, 'I will give it to your descendants.' I have now allowed you to see it with your own eyes, but you will not enter the land." So Moses, the servant of the Lord, died there in the land of Moab, just as the Lord had said. The Lord buried him in a valley near Beth-peor in Moab, but to this day no one knows the exact place. Moses was 120

years old when he died, yet his eyesight was clear, and he was as strong as ever. The people of Israel mourned for Moses on the plains of Moab for thirty days, until the customary period of mourning was over.[52]

The people were allowed to mourn for a designated time and then it was time to get going. Lingering too long in painful places will only steal the joy of our journey. We may suffer and weep but we will also live and find the joy of our journey again.

God promises.

One day, should time continue, my days will come to a conclusion and the passing over will happen for me. I suspect heaven will be more than I imagined and that happy reunions will make it an even more amazing experience than I could have possibly anticipated. I was saved as a very young man in the altar of a small country church my grandfather pastored and my journey has been filled with more joy than pain, more laughter than tears. At times, I've thought life could not have been better than it is and on other days, I've wished to be free from this pain and sorrow that life brings to mankind. All of it is part of the journey we are on. When life is tough, I remind myself that today is just a place where I am—it is not where I'm going. I will get there, if I ***Keep Going!***

The movie *Hercules* by Disney tells the tale of one who seeks to find his place in the world and to understand who he is and what he is meant to be. The theme song *Go the Distance* has always been a favorite of mine. I close with the lyrics and hope they inspire you as they often do me to know that our future is still beyond these moments and that

---

52 Deuteronomy 34:1-8 NLT

in our decisions to continue going on, moving and believing, we will reach the place of our full and complete purpose in God.

> I have often dreamed of a far off place
> Where a hero's welcome will be waiting for me
> Where the crowds will cheer when they see my face
> And a voice keeps saying this is where I'm meant to be
> I'll be there some day I can go the distance
> I will find my way if I can be strong
> I know every mile will be worth my while
> I will go most anywhere to feel like I belong
> Down an unknown road to embrace my fate
> Though that road may wander it will lead me to you
> And a thousand years would be worth the wait
> It might take a lifetime but somehow I'll see it through
> And I won't look back I can go the distance
> And I'll stay on track no I won't accept defeat
> It's an uphill slope but I won't lose hope
> Till I go the distance and my journey is complete.[53]

Just *Keep Going*!

---

53   http://www.stlyrics.com/songs/d/disney6472/icangothedistancehercules246652.html

WHAT OTHERS ARE SAYING ABOUT *KEEP GOING . . .*

Curiosity got me started in this book; great insight kept me reading; hope has me planning on reading it again! Bill Isaacs takes the mystery out of "how to" when it comes to overcoming hard circumstances to embrace the future and destiny . . . Brilliant stuff!

David E. Ramirez, ADVOCATE FOR TRASCENDENT
LEADEARSHIP/CHANGE, LATIN AMERICA

In *Keep Going . . . Handling the Next Big Steps of Your Life*, author Bill Isaacs says, "The lure of remaining in places of comfort and security can be strong and we all have battled the temptation to just stay where we are and never go further." Painting on the canvas of his own personal loss, Isaacs takes us on a journey toward the discovery of God's ultimate plan. He urges us not to languish in the place of comfort but to keep going toward the future God has planned for us. Poignant and thought-provoking, this book will challenge you to embrace the potential of the future to which God is calling you.

Mark L. Williams, GENERAL OVERSEER—
CHURCH OF GOD (Cleveland, TN)

This noble writing by the author is a masterpiece for church leaders and anyone who senses destiny calling. The Old Timers would say, *Keep on, keeping on,* instead of "Keep Going" but the message is the same. Bill eloquently states that God knows what lies ahead because He knows the ending of your life from its beginning. This gives us an indisputable mandate to *Keep Going.*

Wallace J. Sibley, Th.D. ASSISTANT GENERAL
OVERSEER, CHURCH OF GOD (Cleveland, TN)

Someone said, *We live in a microwave society; our present culture demands instant, push-button gratification.* I believe that. It seems we have become a generation of sprinters, instead of distance runners. In his latest work, *Keep Going*, Bill Isaacs addresses the need for patience, steadiness and endurance. These three things require faith, hope and trust in God's plan for our life. It all boils down to this—regardless; it's not optional, ***Keep Going!***

M. Thomas Propes, SECRETARY
GENERAL—CHURCH OF GOD (Cleveland, TN)

Keep Going is a friendly nudge from God that there is hope after loss. It has been said that life isn't fair, Bill reminds us that life is what you make of it after you experience that reality.

Tony Cooper, ADMINISTRATIVE BISHOP NORTH
CENTRAL REGION—MINOT, NORTH DAKOTA

Bill Isaacs doesn't understand *backward*. He is so intent on forward progress and forward advancement it is unlikely that he ever uses the *reverse* gear in his personal vehicle or a golf cart! He has been determined to press on and embrace the future as long as I have known him, even when it was difficult. This most recent of a number of his successful books will challenge you to observe and learn from the life of several Biblical personalities and how God did not intend for us to be *rearview mirror* people but rather *windshield* people. As usual, your mind, heart, and emotions will be touched and dared by the author to become all that God truly intended for you to be. Once you scan the preface or start reading chapter one, you will certainly want to ***Keep Going***!

B. Randall Parris, INTERNATIONAL COORDINATOR, YOUTH/DISCIPLESHIP—CHURCH OF GOD

Keep Going is a journey through life's complexities . . . an insightful navigation through gradations and chapters of life. A compelling READ engaging head and heart...Bill Isaacs draws from his personal experience and professional training to shed light on moving forward through the big steps of our lives...

J. David Stephens, ASSISTANT GENERAL OVERSEER—CHURCH OF GOD

Bill Isaacs is a gifted writer and has a deep understanding of God's word. In his book, *Keep Going . . . Handling the Next BIG Steps of Your Life*, he shares Biblical truths and scriptural principles for overcoming and successful Christian living today taken from the lessons of Scripture. Not only is he a Biblical scholar, but also he has *walked the walk* and he obeyed God and moved forward at a time in his life when he had to have felt that all was gone when he lost his beloved wife. Bill discovered the principles and insights he relates first hand and after deep personal pain. He shares with us, after his own personal journey and revelation, *"the moments and experiences of our past have only positioned us for what is to come! One step, one day, one faithful obedience at a time!"*

David M. Griffis, ASSISTANT GENERAL
OVERSEER—CHURCH OF GOD (Cleveland, TN)